GW01464474

Teacher Education In and For Uncertain Times

Deborah Heck · Angelina Ambrosetti
Editors

Teacher Education In and For Uncertain Times

A·T·E·A
Australian
Teacher Education
Association

Springer

Editors
Deborah Heck
University of the Sunshine Coast
Maroochydore DC, QLD
Australia

Angelina Ambrosetti
Central Queensland University
Noosaville, QLD
Australia

ISBN 978-981-10-8647-2   ISBN 978-981-10-8648-9   (eBook)
https://doi.org/10.1007/978-981-10-8648-9

Library of Congress Control Number: 2018933507

Printed on acid-free paper

This Springer imprint is published by the registered company Springer Nature Singapore Pte Ltd.
part of Springer Nature
The registered company address is: 152 Beach Road, #21-01/04 Gateway East, Singapore 189721,
Singapore

Foreword

This volume is the third collaboration between the Australian Teacher Education Association (ATEA) and Springer published to coincide with ATEA's annual conference. This volume is particularly notable because it includes contributions from New Zealand, marking the inaugural joint conference of ATEA and the Teacher Education Forum of Aotearoa New Zealand (TEFANZ) in July 2018.

The theme of the 2018 conference is 'Teacher Education In and For Uncertain Times.' Arguably, teacher education has never enjoyed particularly certain times regarding its policy and practice frameworks in Australia and New Zealand. However, as this book goes to press, policy shifts in both Australia and New Zealand continue to promise 'interesting' times ahead. The Australian federal government has just announced cuts of over $2 billion to the university sector, and the New Zealand government has just resolved to discontinue its program of national standards for the reporting of school student progress. These initiatives will inevitably have an impact on curriculum and pedagogies in initial and continuing teacher education.

Schools, early childhood services, teacher education providers, families, and students are also acutely aware of wider uncertainties arising from shifts in the global economy, geopolitical relationships, employment futures, technology, climate, and gender roles and relationships. Teacher educators have a particular responsibility to be aware of and respond to these uncertainties so that graduating teachers are equipped to work with diverse learners and diverse learning needs in positive ways. Amidst potentially dystopian views of contemporary society and its immediate future, teacher education, schools, and early childhood services remain sites where positive social futures can be imagined and created.

The authors in this volume were challenged to think about how teacher education can retain this optimism and creativity in the face of uncertain futures. This is an international project. Australian and New Zealand teacher educators closely watch shifts in countries with similar histories of teacher education, such as the US and the UK, and anticipate that some of the policy moves evident there will make their way to Australia. In these countries, there is an increasing mix of public and private interests in teacher education provision and a growing variety of alternatives to traditional school–university partnership structures for the education of teachers. Yet, despite this appearance of growing diversity, the teaching profession continues to be highly regulated around the world, with regulation functioning as a mechanism for governing teachers' work.

This regulatory urge on the part of governments is a timely reminder of the power of teachers' work and its critical role in the making and remaking of cultural norms and expectations. It also explains why initial teacher education, in particular, is so frequently subject to scrutiny and critique by the political class. The recommendations of reviews of teacher education in both Australia and New Zealand in recent years are now playing out, following from *Action Now: Classroom Ready Teachers* in Australia and *Future Focused Initial Teacher Education* in New Zealand. Despite the fanfare accompanying these reports, each with their call for a new, future-focused teaching profession, their recommendations mainly perpetuate the long history of technocratic debates about 'school–university partnerships' and 'the theory–practice divide.'

Despite the intensive scrutiny, regulation, and other constraints, the most cursory glimpse of teacher education research and scholarship suggest a great many teacher educators remain committed to developing counter oppressive curriculum and pedagogy, and to imagining teacher education otherwise. Also, new technologies and forms of social media offer teacher educators new avenues for engagement as public academics and in public spaces. These conversations contribute to wider social movements that are rapidly developing and aspiring to positive social futures, many of which are communitarian in orientation, such as experiments with Universal Basic Income, shifts in the definition of marriage in relation to historical norms, and calls to reclaim resources that were historically part of the commons, such as land, water, and human reproduction.

At the heart of these aspirations is a desire for a more just and equitable distribution of the world's resources. Crucially, these resources include the opportunity to benefit from education. Perhaps the most profound challenge facing teacher education in the immediate term is the need to design programs of initial education and continuing professional learning that equip teachers to raise the achievement of all learners. A greater imaginative effort is required than that evident in recent reviews of teacher education. This effort will necessarily be collaborative and needs to reach beyond the boundaries of teacher education and the teaching profession for inspiration for alternative possibilities. The chapters in this volume, and ongoing research and advocacy by members of ATEA and TEFANZ are welcome contributions to this collaboration.

Melbourne   Joce Nuttall
                                                                      ATEA President 2016–2018

Contents

Editors and Contributors

About the Editors

Deborah Heck is an Associate Professor and the Portfolio Leader Postgraduate and Research Higher Degree programs in the School of Education at the University of the Sunshine Coast. She is engaged in research that explores participation and change in education using a sociocultural lens. This work includes contributions in initial teacher education that explore partnerships between universities and schools that promote successful learning outcomes for graduates. A commissioned teaching and learning grant to review the development of teacher identity and readiness for the profession. Contributions in school contexts, through a completed ARC linkage project, examined the development of a school renewal tool that supports teachers, administrators, students, and parent conversations that mediate change in school. Finally, contributions to higher education involve publications that report on mediated processes for curriculum and assessment alignment and redesign.

Angelina Ambrosetti is a Senior Lecturer and Head of Course in the School of Education and the Arts at Central Queensland University. She is an experienced primary school teacher and taught in Queensland primary schools for 16 years before her move to initial teacher education, where she works with undergraduate preservice teachers in pedagogical practices, and designs and coordinates in school professional practice experiences. Her doctoral research focussed on developing an alternative mentoring model for preservice teachers and their mentors during the professional practice experience. Her ongoing research interests include mentoring in preservice teacher education, mentoring in workplace learning, the professional practice experience in initial teacher education, and professional development for teachers.

Contributors

Angelina Ambrosetti Central Queensland University, Noosaville, QLD, Australia

Peter Anderson Queensland University of Technology, Brisbane, QLD, Australia

Renee Chapman Queensland University of Technology, Brisbane, QLD, Australia

Donella J. Cobb The University of Waikato, Hamilton, New Zealand

Daniel Couch The University of Auckland, Auckland, New Zealand

Anna Darling Monash University, Melbourne, VIC, Australia

Fiona Ell The University of Auckland, Auckland, New Zealand

Jenna Gillett-Swan Queensland University of Technology, Brisbane, QLD, Australia

Deanna Grant-Smith Queensland University of Technology, Brisbane, QLD, Australia

Lexie Grudnoff The University of Auckland, Auckland, New Zealand

Mavis Haigh The University of Auckland, Auckland, New Zealand

Deborah Heck University of the Sunshine Coast, Sippy Downs, QLD, Australia

Mary F. Hill The University of Auckland, Auckland, New Zealand

Kerry Howells University of Tasmania, Hobart, TAS, Australia

Suzanne Hudson Southern Cross University, Gold Coast, QLD, Australia

Amanda Isaac Southern Cross University, Lismore, NSW, Australia

Laura King Murdoch University, Perth, WA, Australia

Caroline Mansfield Murdoch University, Perth, WA, Australia

Lyn McDonald University of Auckland, Auckland, New Zealand

Sharon McDonough Federation University Australia, Mt. Helen, VIC, Australia

Lisa Papatraianou Charles Darwin University, Adelaide, SA, Australia

Ruth Radford University of Tasmania, Hobart, TAS, Australia

Jennifer Rennie Monash University, Melbourne, VIC, Australia

Simone White Queensland University of Technology, Brisbane, QLD, Australia

John Williamson University of Tasmania, Hobart, TAS, Australia

Laura de Zwaan Queensland University of Technology, Brisbane, QLD, Australia

Chapter 1
Reclaiming Educator Professionalism in and for Uncertain Times

Deborah Heck and Angelina Ambrosetti

Abstract Uncertainty in education and teacher education is a certainty in the current international policy context. One of the challenges within this constant process of change and focus on providing evidence of effectiveness is retaining our attention on the purpose of education. Gert Biesta challenges us to reclaim teacher professionalism and engage in discussion about education and its purposes in the context of schooling. Our challenge in this book is to explore and reflect on implications within teacher education and the ways research and scholarship contribute to this discussion. Through reflection on Biesta's (Eur J Educ 50: 1, p. 75–87, 2015) three functions of education qualification, socialisation and subjectification, we aim to engage teacher educators, mentor teachers, school administrators, in-service teachers and pre-service teachers in discussions about the purposes of education. The volume contributes towards discussions about what good education is, and our reflections explore how scholarship provides a space where educators can reclaim their professionalism. Educators across all sectors need to engage in discussion to provide solid justifications for their actions in taking forward education and education research in their context with the aim of making a positive contribution to society. The chapter explores the positive contributions teacher education is making to this debate and identifies ways we can reclaim democratic professionalisms with implications for policy, practice and research.

Keywords Professionalism · Teacher education · Reform · Change · Uncertainty

D. Heck (✉)
University of the Sunshine Coast, Sippy Downs, QLD, Australia
e-mail: dheck@usc.edu.au

A. Ambrosetti
Central Queensland University, Noosaville, QLD, Australia
e-mail: a.ambrosetti@cqu.edu.au

© Springer Nature Singapore Pte Ltd. 2018
D. Heck and A. Ambrosetti (eds.), *Teacher Education In and For Uncertain Times*,
https://doi.org/10.1007/978-981-10-8648-9_1

1

Introduction

The way we live, the way we work, the way we communicate and socialise in these contemporary times are influenced by the increasing and changing globalisation of our world. Globalisation links and interconnects individual nations and world systems through economic, cultural and political dimensions (Marginson, 1999; Singh, 2004). The policies developed and implemented and the professions in which they are situated are impacted by the globalisation of our communities in ways we could not have predicted in the past. However, as Dale (1999, p. 2) asserts, 'the nature and impact of globalisation effects vary enormously across different countries, according to their position in the world and regional economies'.

Of particular interest in this chapter is the impact of globalisation on policy in teacher education. We are interested in how the economic, cultural and political dimensions of individual nations are impacted by globalisation, and how this translates into education policy. Interestingly, despite different cultural contexts and the economic, political and social variables associated with the historical development of education in contemporary times, educational policy in many countries, particularly with respect to teacher education, have become increasingly similar. However, Lingard, Rawolle and Taylor (2005) argue that the educational policy landscape is 'multi-layered, stretching from the local to the global' (p. 76).

Uncertainty in the teacher education context as an outcome of globalisation is an increasing field of literature internationally with many researchers searching for answers. Singh, Kenway and Apple (2007) in their analysis of the impact of globalisation on education policy use Falk's categorisation of 'globalisation from above' and 'globalisation from below', to begin to debate and make sense of the topic (p. 2). The category of 'globalisation from above' considers policy as a top-down approach whereby a corporation or government develops and implements policy as they see fit. As such, this may occur with minimal consultation or input from those who will be directly involved in enacting policy at the ground level. In contrast, 'globalisation from below' considers policy from the ground up and is developed and implemented through immersion in the context. This categorisation considers the moral ground, and although it does not discount globalisation, it takes into account the place, space, cultures, identities and relationships of the context. Although the categorisations of globalisation offered by M. Singh and colleagues do not reflect the complexity of globalisation (Lingard et al., 2005; Singh et al., 2007), they offer an avenue in which we can start unpacking policy, practice and research.

This volume considers the role of initial and continuing teacher education in uncertain times. It elaborates principles and practices of teacher education that maintain curiosity and optimism about the potential of teacher education and about the manifold achievements of pre-service and in-service teachers. It reports the work of teacher education researchers who are engaging with how teacher education can prepare teachers committed to counter-oppressive curriculum and pedagogy and reflects the critical role of teacher educators as professionals and public academics.

Uncertainty and Teacher Education

Teacher education internationally faces uncertain times. The provision of teacher education is increasingly diversified across public and private interests, and reviews of teacher education in several countries have continued to question its efficacy and impact. In the Australian and New Zealand teacher education contexts, for example, recent reviews and directions for initial teacher education (ITE) such as the *Action Now: Classroom Ready Teachers* report (Teacher Education Ministerial Advisory Group, 2014) and the *Future Focused Initial Teacher Education* vision (Education Council, 2017) are illustrations of government focus on efficacy and impact. At the core of reforms such as these is the focus on ensuring quality teaching practices that in turn enable quality learning outcomes for students in schools (Ambrosetti, Capeness, Kriewaldt, & Rorrison, 2018). Although such reviews and their associated reforms create uncertainty, they also provide the opportunity to rethink and engage in professional discourse about the profession and what quality means in education and teaching. Uncertainty prompts us to know and do differently.

Biesta (2017, p. 315) describes education today as being in the 'age of measurement' whereby the performance of schools, the students within schools, national education systems and universities that offer teacher education programmes are valued through measurement of effectiveness and achievement. Global educational measurement strategies such as the Organisation for Economic Co-operation and Development's (OECD) programme for International Student Achievement (PISA) is a prominent example of a measure that has a significant impact on education policy at a national level. PISA results, in many countries, have had a direct impact on the review and reform of teacher education and the profession of teaching. The basis for using measurement scores such as PISA to inform education policy by governments is a prime example of 'globalisation from above' that fuels uncertainty. In addition, Rowe and Skourdoumbis (2017, p. 3) assert that 'education reforms seek to establish a problem that needs to be fixed'. They draw on Blackmore and Lauder (2004, p. 22) to identify that problem setting is often the focus of processes that connect with unquestioned logic rather than problem-solving in education. Thus contributing to uncertainty, as governments typically identify problems that have technical solutions (Rowe & Skourdoumbis, 2017).

In the Australian context, reform is based on the problem of lack of classroom readiness of teacher education graduates. As a response to lower global rankings in PISA, the quality of classroom teacher graduates has become the focus of reform and classroom readiness has become the key policy driver. However, both Gore (2015) and Rowe and Skourdoumbis (2017) identify the term classroom readiness as missing a clear definition and conceptualisation. Hence, educators lack a shared understanding of what it means, making it difficult to respond to the reform agenda.

New Zealand is also in the midst of change with a new vision for teacher education recently announced (Education Council, 2017). Key aspects of strengthened ITE programmes include a focus on the use of teaching standards to ensure that beginning teachers are ready for the classroom, raised selection and entry requirements, as well as a focus on partnerships between ITE and learning settings to improve the quality of professional experience (Education Council, 2017).

In the United States (USA), the college and university system of teacher preparation has been deemed a failure with strong debate surrounding the issue about what teachers need to know and be able to do, who should become a teacher and how prospective teachers should be prepared (Zeichner, Payne, & Brayko, 2015). However, 'whose knowledge should count in teacher education' is identified as a missing component of the debate (p. 123). The debate and uncertainty occurring in the USA have similarities to the Australian context, including concern around student achievement and the skills and knowledge of graduate teachers.

The UK has also experienced policy review and reform in recent times. Aubrey and Bell (2017) report on significant changes in the period from 2000 to 2010 whereby a major overhaul of teacher education occurred. They identified many positive features of the reform agenda in the UK. However, they also identified the impact of uncertainty across the numerous reforms and policies implemented. Like the Australian and US examples, the focus of the reforms was on the knowledge and skills of beginning teachers and their ability to facilitate successful student learning achievements. Globalisation from above with little consultation from below occurred in the UK context.

Although the examples above demonstrate how reforms in teacher education have created uncertain times for pre-service teachers, the reform also impacts in-service teachers and teacher educators (Aubrey & Bell, 2017). Teacher educators are more often than not at the battlefront of change and thus are immersed in the uncertainty that change in policy creates. They implement change in and through initial teacher education programmes that consequently explicitly impact the pre-service teachers enrolled in those programmes. In this respect, they also inexplicitly impact schools and in-service teachers and the role that they play as pre-service teachers undertake professional experience. Partnerships between universities and schools are under increasing scrutiny, and collaborative processes during such aspects of ITE as the professional experience are seen to be key in the development of the knowledge, skills and professionalism of the next generation of teachers (Ambrosetti et al., 2018).

Two key themes can be identified from the reforms that are occurring all over the world. Entry pathways into initial teacher education and questioning who can become a teacher are the first theme within the examples of reform. The use of professional standards to make judgements about the competency of both pre-service teachers and in-service teachers is a second key theme. The assessment of pre-service teachers throughout their ITE programme is increasingly subject to assessments of their performance. The implementation of a teacher performance assessment (TPA) task in Australia, in particular, has prompted a rethink of programme structure, the development of teaching knowledge and skills and the ongoing assessment of pre-service teachers.

Practising teachers also face new and uncertain challenges related to new regulatory demands, funding models, policy frameworks and regimes of assessment that foster competition, rather than collaboration, between educators. Young people across education contexts are growing up in an era of rapidly increasing social inequality, where problems of opportunity and achievement persist for many groups, amidst discourses of 'post-truth' and 'fake news'.

Despite the fact that the structure of schools and the delivery of education have undergone minimal change over time, change in the field of teacher education is rapid and rigorous, bringing uncertainty to both the profession and also those who engage with the profession. Education reform, however, should not be viewed from a negative stance, as uncertainty can enable us to incorporate change in innovative ways (Ambrosetti et al., 2018). The chapters in this volume are an opportunity to demonstrate innovation and change in teacher education in uncertain times and explore the role of teacher educators as professionals.

Reclaiming Educator Professionalism

What does it mean to be a teacher education professional in uncertain times? Interestingly, there is little agreement in the literature about the definition of the term profession or professional. Professions seem to have three key features: specialised knowledge of some form, a level of autonomous self-government that monitors ethical practice and they are performed in service to others (Bair, 2016). While teaching meets the requirements identified above as a profession, it is not always considered equivalent to other professions such as law, medicine or engineering (Bahr & Mellor, 2016). However, it needs to be acknowledged that views of professionalism have changed over time with Hargreaves (2000) identifying four common ages: pre-professional, autonomous professional, collegial professional and post-professional in many Anglophone nations. In the light of the uncertainty and education reform agenda we have outlined, there is a need to heed the call from Hargreaves (2000, p. 176) that 'If teachers want to become professionally stronger, they must now open themselves up and become more publicly vulnerable and accessible'. Recent scholarship by Bair (2016) identified educators' views of professionalism were restricted, thus highlighting the importance of the call for teachers and teacher educators to reclaim professionalism. The restricted view was in stark contrast to the activist professional view of social work students and faculty identified in Bair's comparative study.

As educators, we need to reclaim the definition of professional in the post-professional stage (Hargreaves, 2000). Evans (2008, p. 29) provides a useful reframing of the notion of professionalism to support these efforts:

> Professionality-influenced practice that is consistent with commonly-held consensual delineations of a specific profession and that both contributes to and reflects perceptions of the professions' purpose and status and the specific nature, range and levels of service provided by, and expertise prevalent within, the profession, as well as the general ethical code underpinning this practice.

The challenge of enacting this definition in education is identifying how to enhance professionality in teacher education. Biesta suggests that educators take the time to reflect on what it means to be a professional in the context of education (2015, 2017). He suggests that we need to reclaim the definition of professionalism by rejecting and reframing many of the commonly held beliefs about education. Beliefs are often connected to what Evans (2008) refers to as the 'required' or 'prescribed' views of education professionality rather than 'enacted' practice. One of the challenges of reclaiming this space is the lack of teacher and teacher education voices in public discussion and development of teaching quality and standards (Bahr & Mellor, 2016). However, in making a move to reclaim professionalism, we need to take professional actions that move our work towards discussions about how our work contributes to the purposes of education. We should consider our work in this space as part of the 'globalisation from below' in the context of current education reforms as 'globalisation from above'.

Biesta (2015) argues that there are three purposes of education that make education a multidimensional field. The three dimensions are qualifications, socialisations and subjectification. Qualifications are related to the development of the ability to do something regarding vocational outcomes as well as the ability to engage generally in life. Socialisation as a purpose introduces students to the traditions of society cultural, political and social. While subjectification refers to the impact education has on the person that impact can be positive or negative. The three domains are connected and work together, for example increased knowledge (qualification) leads to an understanding of cultural practices (socialisation) and increased capacity to take action on an issue (subjectification). However, not all impacts are positive. Hence, too much emphasis on one domain, for example, increased performance on standardised tests (qualifications) can have a negative impact on student and teacher well-being and motivations to engage (subjectification).

As educators working across these three domains in uncertain times, we respond to a range of shifts in our professional practice that may at first glance seem to be a move towards a more democratic education. However, Biesta (2017) asserts that there are three aspects that require reframing if we are to move towards a more democratic form of professionalism. The first reframing is a move away from the view of students as customers. The view undermines the professional role of educator. Biesta (2017) suggests that an educator's professional role is to engage with students to identify what is needed, rather than just to provide what they might already have identified they want. If education as a profession is just engaged in delivering the wants of those seeking education, then a very limited view of professionalism emerges. Our challenge is to identify how to reimagine the dialogue that is required between educators and students to engage in a more democratic approach to education. The second reframing is a shift away from managerial approaches to accountability. Mandated standards or quality requirements are an example of managerial accountability. In this context, the actions of the profession are compared to the mandated standards rather than the quality of professional actions by teachers and their contribution to the education of students and society. The managerial approach to accountability identifies a shift in both who defines the quality of the profession and who the professional is accountable to. The third and final reframing is the privileging of evidenced-based practice over professional judgement. The emphasis on the use of only educational practices that have a clear evidence base typically identified as 'best practice' limits professionalism. The use of a limited range of proven strategies that 'work' does not allow for educators to make professional judgements about context.

Based on the definition of professionalism provided by Evans (2008), we are called as teacher educators to engage with an exploration of teacher education practice and schooling. Also, Biesta (2017) asserts that teacher educators should identify the needs of their students and seek to establish authority in education contexts. We emphasise that as educators this work is part of our role across teaching, research, scholarship, administration and service. If we are to reclaim our democratic professional role as educators, we need to consider how we are engaging with the exploration and definition of teacher education practice and schooling. This conversation and dialogue need to be ongoing to avoid the process of reducing teaching to a technical vocation. In developing a democratic dialogic engagement with our students, we can take on the professional role of defining and redefining the educational purposes for both the individual and the collective. It is our role to explore with students democracy as 'a process in which the "wants" and desires of individuals are brought into collective deliberation in order to figure which of those wants and desires can legitimately be "carried" by the collective' (Biesta, 2017, p. 327). Further, our role as researchers working in universities is to explore through research and scholarship this ongoing dialogue.

The purpose of this volume is threefold. To reflect on current research in the context of teacher education and consider how our work contributes to the development of scholarship related to the purposes of education qualifications, socialisation, and subjectification. To explore how educators participate in scholarship that develops our ability to engage with the identification of individual and collective student needs in teacher education. And additionally, to recognise ways that educators have established authority in their education contexts as democratic professionals. Our reflections on current teacher education scholarship will provide an opportunity for considering the contribution of current research, identify scope for further research and explore the implications for policy and practice. We aim to maintain an open dialogue and be mindful of the narrowing effect of the dominance of contemporary policy language (Biesta, Priestley, & Robinson, 2017) as we engage in this reflection.

Reflections on Contemporary Teacher Education Contributions

Each of the chapters in this volume highlights the uncertainty that is apparent in teacher education contexts in Australia and New Zealand that have occurred through policy reform agendas. It is important to note that whilst the chapters' highlight uncertainty, each chapter offers confidence that an alternative way of doing and knowing is possible. The chapters also highlight the 'collective other' that has emerged as a result of the reform agenda in teacher education: university academics, pre-service teachers, mentor teachers and school administrators working together to ensure changes in policy are successful for those students at the centre of such reforms. Matters of teacher qualification and programme accreditation also are a reoccurring theme in a number of chapters. In saying this, the chapters bring to light three key areas that teacher educators are concerned about in contemporary times. As such, the chapters highlight issues and concerns for pre-service teachers, mentor teachers and teacher educators, about professional experience, the impact of ITE on graduate teacher knowledge and skills, workforce needs and how the application of practice occurs. Each chapter demonstrates one or more aspect of Biesta's (2017) purposes of education.

Professional Experience

In Chap. 2, Grant-Smith, Zwaan, Chapman and Gillett-Swan document key findings from their research about how financial stress can and does impact on educational experiences for students during the professional experience component of their programme. The chapter provides a challenge for teacher educators to consider ways to understand and respond to student needs in the context of their placements. How might the educational policies and processes value more equally the qualifications, socialisation and subjectification identified by Biesta (2015)? Teacher educators are called to engage in ongoing dialogue and debate with students, teacher educators and placement staff, university support staff, professional experience sites, employers, education departments and accreditation bodies to explore ways to focus on the purposes of teacher education and discuss opportunities for innovation and change in professional experience.

Issac and Hudson in Chap. 4 open up space for discussion about supervising teacher's role as teacher educators in working with student teachers during professional experience. The research engages with supervising teachers' views of assessing student teachers using the mandated professional standards. Engagement in dialogue with supervising teachers underpinned by symbolic interactionism provides a rich data source that identifies the complexity and competing identities supervising teachers bring to the role. The challenges of balancing the purposes of education in their context, including Biesta's notion of qualifications, socialisation and subjectification, seem to permeate the data. It highlights the challenges confronting supervising teachers in their role as teacher educators and the way professional standards are identified as undermining their professionalism. The outcomes of the research suggest some examples of how this work might be further developed to provide opportunities for more democratic notions of teacher educator professionalism to emerge.

Radford, Howells and Williamson also explore the voice of mentor teachers in schools with a focus on what is involved in teaching about teaching in challenging school settings in Chap. 5. The findings regarding responsibility for teaching student teachers connect to Biesta's reflections on the purposes of education and move us away from the unhelpful notion that the purpose of education is student learning in isolation. These findings connect well with the view that 'the point of education is that student learns something, that they learn it for a reason, and they learn it from someone' (Biesta, 2015, p. 76). Recommendations for professional development for mentor teachers and university academic engagement with mentor teachers aligned with the findings from Chap. 4. The development of further standards specifically for the mentor teacher role is also suggested in this chapter. However, this suggestion is framed alongside a caution regarding regulation and accountability.

Initial Teacher Education Programmes

Cobb and Couch in Chap. 3 explore global competence and the increasing role of international organisations in the process of initial teacher education qualifications and influence on pedagogic governance. The chapter provides an analysis of the implications of the emerging global competence assessment of secondary students internationally using Basil Bernstein as a theoretical tool. The chapter provides ample scope for teacher educator agency. We are challenged to engage as professionals and work with our students to explore the implication of globalisation on education. The authors suggest Comparative and International Education as one useful approach for undertaking this exploration in their context, and we welcome further research in this space in the future. The analysis provides useful understandings for each of us as teacher educators to analyse the needs of our own students and forge teaching and learning partnerships that will provide both students and academic staff agency in this space.

In Chap. 8, Rennie, White, Anderson and Darling challenge teacher educators to reflect on how programmes of study prepare teacher education students for their future roles working in rural and remote communities in Australia. Finding a place within the ITE curriculum for this work to be undertaken beyond the implementation of the requirements of the professional standards for teachers is a challenge in Australia and internationally. Developing meaningful educational experiences in rural and remote settings is thought-provoking work and requires the engagement of all the partners in a collaborative way to identify and develop the entire process. One example of space for collaboration identified in the research was curriculum. The authors suggest making a shift away from pre-identified learning outcomes and considering the teaching opportunities in rural and remote professional experiences. Maintaining a focus on the needs of the student teachers, school students, teachers, administrators and community members is an important consideration and challenge for the development of flexible and responsive curriculum.

Ell, Grudnoff, Haigh and Hill explore the issues for teacher educators connected with the requirements to develop school university partnerships. Chapter 9 explores how engagement in a collaborative research partnership exploring equity-centred teaching provided opportunities outside of typical professional experience partnerships to develop a deeper dialogue that engages schools and university staff in discussions about the purposes of education. Exploring the practice for equity facets required practitioners to engage in dialogue to enact their meaning in practice. The project identified a social space for engagement in the knowledge and skills of teaching. There was a focus on orientation to the practice of teaching by the mentor teachers. The teacher educators were acknowledged as possessing authority and as a consequence, there was a change to the power relationships in the professional experience context when working with teacher mentors. This change was evidence because of shifts in the teacher mentor practice for equity across all three of Biesta's purposes of education qualification, socialisation and subjectification.

Application to Practice

In Chap. 6, Mansfield, Paparaianou, McDonough and King explore teacher educator views regarding student teacher resilience. A contribution that connects teacher educator work delivering qualifications with resilience as a critical mechanism for sustained effectiveness and growth for educators. This connects closely with the socialisation and subjectification purpose of education identified by Biesta (2015). The challenges of standardisation of teacher quality by the development and monitoring of standards are noted as lacking a connection to the contextual nature of teaching. Recent developments that seek to test non-cognitive capabilities before entry to teacher education programmes in Australia create uncertain times. There seems to be uncertainty about the testing process that creates uncertainty for those seeking to enter the profession. The research suggests that while there are barriers to implementation, there are opportunities for teacher educators to engage with resilience in their own contexts and drawing on the work of Biesta (2017) to reclaim their professionalism for themselves and their students. The work suggests the incorporation of resilience into the professional standards while also identifying the cautionary tale of the impact of standards on the profession.

McDonald in Chap. 7 explores the challenge teacher educators face working in partnership with associate teachers and students to negotiate professional experience. It was encouraging to see in this context that the students were identified as 'students' rather than the learners and the teachers, both teacher educators and associated teachers, were required to play an active role in identifying and refining learning. The explicit teaching and use of the self-regulatory practices provided an opportunity for these teacher educators to authentically engage students in a high-stakes qualifications context with both socialisation and subjectification purposes of education (Biesta, 2017). The teacher educators in this example identify the space for the discussion, engage students with reflection on what their own needs are and then work with teacher associates and students to refine the identification of needs. What is important here is that they work in collaboration with the associate teachers to support students to explore what they need to do to achieve the qualification and how they can use the social structures and reflection along with their agency and motivation to engage in the education process. A challenge identified by the author in this context is that this was not the experience for all students, rather it was the experience of those with dedicated teacher educators concerned about engaging with their students on their placement. What did seem to be evident from the voices of the student's in Chap. 7 was students who engaged in these triad conversations with associate teachers and teacher educators had a transformative experience.

The ideas, issues and research presented in each chapter provide a starting point and are by no means the end point of the conversation. As such, the chapters enable the continued development of collective agency of our work as educators. The authors of each chapter recommend that further research is needed to be undertaken so that we can continue the dialogue about teacher education, its purposes and the practices associated with it.

Conclusion

As you read this text, we encourage you to consider ways that you can lay claim to your professionalism as an educator involved in teacher education in a myriad of different ways. You should take heart that there is clear evidence of teacher educators engaging as democratic professionals in response to teacher education reforms in the UK. Aubrey and Bell (2017, p. 108) identify that 'teacher educators adapted critical practices to conform in a flexible, and when called for, covert and even subversive manner' based on their democratic and personal philosophical values. The challenge as teacher educators is to heed the call to engage in the conversation with all participants about the purpose of education, to identify what those involved in education need to learn not just what they might want to learn and to work in ways that allow students give authority to all those engaged as teacher educators.

We would like to acknowledge this text as an opportunity for educators to engage in the dialogue to reclaim professionalism. The Australian Teacher Education Association (ATEA) and Teacher Education Forum of Aotearoa New Zealand (TEFANZ) make a valuable contribution to these debates by providing opportunities for teacher educators to collaborate through the development of this book and engagement at conferences and workshops. Consider as you read the breadth of ways teacher educators are engaging with uncertain times and how you might extend your own professionalism.

References

Ambrosetti, A., Capeness, R., Kriewaldt, J., & Rorrison, D. (2018). Educating future teachers: Insights, conclusions and challenges. In J. Kriewaldt, A. Ambrosetti, D. Rorrison, & R. Capeness (Eds.), *Educating teachers: Innovative perspectives in professional experience* (pp. 235–244). Singapore: Springer.

Aubrey, K., & Bell, L. (2017). Teacher education in further education 2000–2010: Subversion, avoidance and compliance. *Journal of Further and Higher Education, 41*(2), 99–111. https://doi.org/10.1080/0309877X.2015.1062846.

Bahr, N., & Mellor, S. (2016). *Building quality in teaching and teacher education.* Melbourne: ACER.

Bair, M. A. (2016). Professionalism: A comparative case study of teachers, nurses, and social workers. *Educational Studies, 42*(5), 450–464. https://doi.org/10.1080/03055698.2016.1219651.

Biesta, G. (2015). What is education for? On good education, teacher judgement, and educational professionalism. *European Journal of Education, 50*(1), 75–87. https://doi.org/10.1111/ejed.12109.

Biesta, G. (2017). Education, Measurement and the Professions: Reclaiming a space for democratic professionality in education. *Educational Philosophy and Theory, 49*(4), 315–330. https://doi.org/10.1080/00131857.2015.1048665.

Biesta, G., Priestley, M., & Robinson, S. (2017). Talking about education: Exploring the significance of teachers' talk for teacher agency. *Journal of Curriculum Studies, 49*(1), 38–54. https://doi.org/10.1080/00220272.2016.1205143.

Blackmore, J., & Lauder, H. (2004). Researching policy. In B. Somekh & C. Lewin (Eds.), *Research methods in the social sciences* (pp. 97–104). London: Sage.

Dale, R. (1999). Specifying globalization effects on national policy: A focus on the mechanisms. *Journal of Education Policy, 14*(1), 1–17. https://doi.org/10.1080/026809399286468.

Education Council. (2017). Initial teacher education 2021 New Zealand. Retrieved from https://www.educationcouncil.org.nz/sites/default/files/ITE%20detail%20decisions%20and%20vision.pdf.

Evans, L. (2008). Professionalism, professionality and the development of education professionals. *British Journal of Educational Studies, 56*(1), 20–38. https://doi.org/10.1111/j.1467-8527.2007.00392.x.

Gore, J. M. (2015). Evidence of impact of teacher education programs: A focus on classroom observation. Retrieved from Melbourne: https://www.aitsl.edu.au/tools-resources/resource/evidence-of-impact-of-teacher-education-programs-a-focus-on-classroom-observation.

Hargreaves, A. (2000). Four ages of professionalism and professional learning. *Teachers and Teaching, 6*(2), 151–182. https://doi.org/10.1080/713698714.

Lingard, B., Rawolle, S., & Taylor, S. (2005). Globalizing policy sociology in education: Working with Bourdieu. *Journal of Education Policy, 20*(6), 759–777. https://doi.org/10.1080/02680930500238945.

Marginson, S. (1999). After globalization: Emerging politics of education. *Journal of Education Policy, 14*(1), 19–31.

Rowe, E. E., & Skourdoumbis, A. (2017). Calling for 'urgent national action to improve the quality of initial teacher education': The reification of evidence and accountability in reform agendas. *Journal of Education Policy, 1–17.* https://doi.org/10.1080/02680939.2017.1410577.

Singh, P. (2004). Globalization and education. *Educational Theory, 54*(1), 103–115.

Singh, M., Kenway, J., & Apple, M. W. (2007). Globalizing education: Perspectives from above and below. In M. W. Apple, J. Kenway, & M. Singh (Eds.), *Globalizing education: Politics, pedagogies, and politics* (pp. 1–29). New York: Peter Lang Publishing.

Teacher Education Ministerial Advisory Group. (2014). Action now: Classroom ready teachers report. Retrieved from https://docs.education.gov.au/system/files/doc/other/action_now_classroom_ready_teachers_print.pdf.

Zeichner, K., Payne, K. A., & Brayko, K. (2015). Democratizing teacher education. *Journal of Teacher Education, 66*(2), 122–135. https://doi.org/10.1177/0022487114560908.

Author Biographies

Deborah Heck is an Associate Professor and the Portfolio Leader Postgraduate and Research Higher Degree programmes in the School of Education at the University of the Sunshine Coast. Debbie is engaged in research that explores participation and change in education using a sociocultural lens. This work includes contributions to initial teacher education that explore partnerships between universities and schools that promote successful learning outcomes for graduates. A commissioned teaching and learning grant reviews to review the development of teacher identity and readiness for the profession. Contributions in school contexts, through a completed ARC linkage project, examined the development of a school renewal tool that supports teachers, administrators, students and parent conversations that mediate change in school. Finally, contributions to higher education involve publications that report on mediated processes for curriculum and assessment alignment and redesign.

Angelina Ambrosetti is a Senior Lecturer and Head of Course in the School of Education and the Arts at Central Queensland University. She is an experienced primary school teacher and taught in Queensland primary schools for 16 years before her move to initial teacher education, where she works with undergraduate preservice teachers in pedagogical practices and designs and coordinates in school professional practice experiences. Angelina's doctoral research focussed on developing an alternative mentoring model for preservice teachers and their mentors during the professional practice experience. Her ongoing research interests include mentoring in preservice teacher education, mentoring in workplace learning, the professional practice experience in initial teacher education and professional development for teachers.

Chapter 2
'It's the Worst, but Real Experience Is Invaluable': Pre-service Teacher Perspectives of the Costs and Benefits of Professional Experience

Deanna Grant-Smith, Laura de Zwaan, Renee Chapman and Jenna Gillett-Swan

Abstract Professional experience, or practicum placements, is an important component in the education of pre-service teachers and preparing them for their own classrooms after graduation. However, while the pedagogical and personal development benefits of participation are well documented, the personal costs of participation have been less comprehensively explored. This chapter identifies the perceived costs and benefits of participation in practicum from the perspective of undergraduate and postgraduate pre-service teachers attending an Australia university. The research study reported in this chapter reveals that the practicum experience is, on the whole, associated with positive feelings and the opportunity to gain practical 'real-world' experience and professional development. However, the financial hardship that can be created or magnified as a consequence of participation in practicum can negatively impact the practicum experience and the well-being of a pre-service teacher. The chapter concludes by reflecting on approaches that universities and accrediting bodies may consider to manage the financial and other impacts of practicum participation on pre-service teachers without decreasing their educational and experiential value.

Keywords Initial teacher education · Practicum · Placement · Financial stress · Professional experience · Field experience

D. Grant-Smith (✉) · L. de Zwaan · R. Chapman · J. Gillett-Swan
Queensland University of Technology, Brisbane, QLD, Australia
e-mail: deanna.grantsmith@qut.edu.au

L. de Zwaan
e-mail: laura.dezwaan@qut.edu.au

R. Chapman
e-mail: renee.chapman@qut.edu.au

J. Gillett-Swan
e-mail: jenna.gillettswan@qut.edu.au

© Springer Nature Singapore Pte Ltd. 2018
D. Heck and A. Ambrosetti (eds.), *Teacher Education In and For Uncertain Times*,
https://doi.org/10.1007/978-981-10-8648-9_2

Introduction and Aims

To satisfy accreditation requirements, Australian education students are required to undertake a range of school-based placements throughout their degree. There is a strong agreement among educational theorists that practicum is a necessary component in the education of teachers (Le Cornu & Ewing, 2008; OECD, 2014; Smith & Lev-Ari, 2005; TEMAG, 2014) and the pedagogy of pre-service teacher education is well-developed. Practicum involves the supervised practical application of theory in a school-based setting (Beck & Kosnick, 2002) to introduce pre-service teachers to the realities of teaching in an authentic but supervised teaching environment. The benefits of practicum participation are widely accepted, with pre-service teacher accounts that pre-service experience in schools is the most beneficial and influential part of teacher preparation, claiming this is when they learned to teach (Smith & Lev-Ari, 2005). Possibly as a result of the evident benefits of such experiences, much of the research on pre-service teacher's experiences of practicum has focused on improving participant learning outcomes and the practical and emotional demands of the teaching profession (Giannakaki, Hobson, & Malderez, 2011; Lawson, Cakmak, Gunduz, & Busher, 2015) or the practicum workplace (e.g. Grudnoff, 2011; Le Cornu & Ewing, 2008; Wilkens, Ashton, Maurer, & Smith, 2015).

Despite the prevalence of practicum in teacher education and its intensive character, the financial pressures associated with practicum for education students remains under-examined relative to other disciplines with high levels of work-integrated learning (Moore, Fern, & Peach, 2012). A focus on the financial hardship experienced by participants during practicum is important as it is a known source of stress and anxiety for tertiary students (Creedon, 2015; Ross, Niebling, & Heckert, 1999) and a common cause of attrition (Schofield, Keane, Fletcher, Shrestha, & Percival, 2009). Financial hardship can negatively impact academic performance (Joo, Durband, & Grable, 2008) and broader well-being (Deasy, Coughlan, Pironom, Jourdan, & Mannis-McNamara, 2014; Watson, Barber, & Dziurawiec, 2015). Recent research in the field of social work (Johnstone, Brough, Crane, Marston, & Correa-Velez, 2016) has highlighted the relationship between unpaid placements and financial hardship which they believe can compromise the practicum learning experience. Financial constraints are a significant source of stress for students required to undertake placements (Timmins & Kaliszer, 2002), on top of the financial pressures students already face (Fosnacht & Calderone, 2017; Harding, 2011; Heckman, Lim, & Monalto, 2014).

This chapter identifies the perceived costs and benefits of participation in practicum from the perspective of undergraduate and postgraduate pre-service teachers in an Australia university. In particular, it highlights the financial hardship created or magnified as a consequence of practicum participation. The chapter concludes by reflecting on approaches that universities and accrediting bodies may consider to reduce the financial impact of practicum participation on pre-service teachers without decreasing their educational value.

Research Approach

This chapter reports on the findings of education respondents from a larger study of practicum experiences funded by the National Centre for Student Equity in Higher Education (Grant-Smith, Gillett-Swan, & Chapman, 2017) in which students in the QUT Faculties of Health and Education enrolled in a practicum unit in 2016 were invited by email to complete an online survey. Ethics approval for the project was provided by QUT. Of the five hundred and fifty-two (552) students who completed the Qualtrics survey to a satisfactory level to be included in the analysis, close to one-third were enrolled in an education degree (31%, n = 172). Online surveys have been successfully applied in studies seeking participant perspectives and experiences of practicum (e.g. Kanno & Koesk, 2010; Spooner-Lane, Tangen, & Campbell, 2007). The survey instrument employed was a refined version of a pilot project which investigated the practicum experiences of a cohort of Graduate Diploma of Education students (Grant-Smith & Gillett-Swan, 2017). The survey included a mix of open and scaled questions. Basic biographical and demographic questions were also included to provide context for responses.

A mixed-methods approach, informed by critical realism (Krauss, 2005), was adopted to analyse the data. Descriptive statistics were prepared, and cross-tabulation was used to generate a range of two-way tables to examine the relationships between variables, which were then analysed using chi-square tests. Descriptive content analysis was used to thematically identify and describe the primary content and meaning within the data obtained from the open-ended survey questions. This resulted in categorising, listing and quantification of themes based on the frequency of occurrence to determine their prominence (Bryman, 2008). Participant quotes are presented in italics and identified by the level of study of the respondent. All respondent quotes are from full-time students unless otherwise indicated.

Pre-service Teacher Perceptions of Practicum

Practicum can be a time of intense learning and considerable stress for participants (Danyluk, 2013). Respondents were asked to identify what they considered to be the best and worst aspects of participation in a practicum placement and the feelings they experienced during placement. The respondent sample was predominantly female (82%, n = 141) with six per cent of respondents (n = 10) choosing not to disclose their gender. Most respondents were domestic students (92%, n = 158) though seven per cent chose not to disclose their citizenship (n = 12). Only three per cent of respondents (n = 5) reported speaking a language other than English at home. As shown in Fig. 2.1, the majority of respondents were aged 30 years and younger (67%, n = 94), with the average age of 27 years for female respondents and 29 years for male respondents. More than a quarter of respondents (28%, n = 48) reported that they had children living at home with them.

21 years & younger	4% n=6		33% n=53
22 – 25 years	3% n=5	19% n=30	
26 – 30 years	2% n=3	11% n=18	
31 – 35 years	2% n=3	5% n=8	
36 – 40 years		6% n=10	
41 – 45 years	1% n=1	7% n=13	
46+ years	2% n=3	5% n=8	

Legend
■ male respondents
□ female respondents

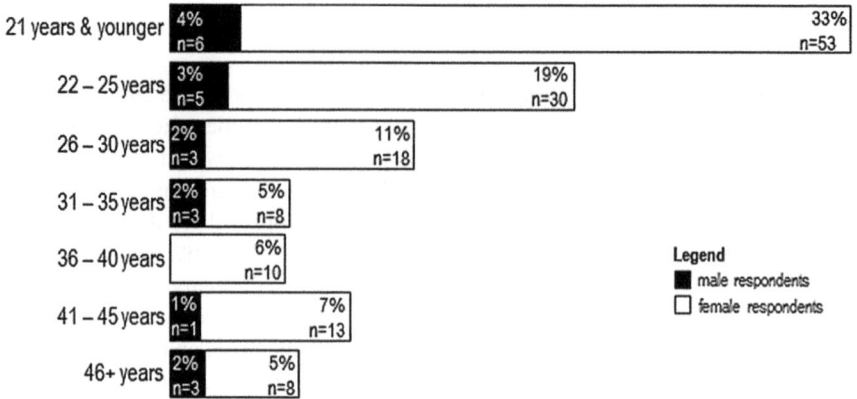

Fig. 2.1 Respondent age profile by gender

Table 2.1 Respondent profile by level of study

Gender	Undergraduate		Postgraduate	
	Number of respondents	*Average age of respondents*	*Number of respondents*	*Average age of respondents*
Female	107	26 years	34	32 years
Male	12	22 years	9	38 years

Undergraduate students dominated the sample (72%, n = 124) with just over a quarter postgraduate (26%, n = 44). As shown in Table 2.1, there is a comparable number of undergraduate and postgraduate male respondents, but more than three times as many undergraduate than postgraduate female respondents. At the time of the survey, the average number of days that a respondent had participated in a practicum placement was 33 days ±23.[1]

The majority of respondents (75%, n = 130) had paid employment, whether that was their main source of income or a supplement source of income. Of the 130 respondents who stated that they were in paid employment, 79% were undergraduate students (n = 103) and 21% were postgraduate students (n = 27). More than three quarters of female respondents (78%, n = 109) and more than two-thirds of male respondents (67%, n = 14) were in paid employment. Further, seven respondents (5%) who chose not to disclose their gender were also in paid employment. Respondents were asked if they had continued, or intended to continue, paid employment during their practicum placement. Of those that responded to this question (n = 24), more than half (58%, n = 14) had ceased, or intended to cease, paid work during the placement. These findings are generally consistent with those of Moore et al. (2012) who found that 72% of applicants for an Australian Collaborative Education

---

[1]It should be noted that at the time of the survey some students were still participating in their practicum placement and that it was the first practicum placement for some respondents.

Network (ACEN) scholarship, which included education students, signalled that they would have to cease paid work as a result of practicum participation.

Feelings Experienced During Placement

Assessing the affective experience of practicum using the experience sampling method, in which respondents are required to record their activities and feelings in real time at random intervals (Krueger & Schkade, 2007), is expensive, disruptive and involves very high levels of participant burden. An effective and less burdensome alternative for respondents is to ask them to recall emotions associated with a recent event (Kahneman, Kreuger, Schkade, Schwarz, & Stone, 2004a). We asked respondents to rate the feelings they experienced during practicum participation as an average of their total practicum experience. Table 2.2 shows the average rating given by respondents (n = 171) for each feeling. The rating is from 0 to 100. A rating of 0 would reflect no experience of the feeling during practicum, while a rating of 100 would indicate that the feeling was very prominent during the practicum. The feelings measured were derived from Kahneman, Kreuger, Schkade, Schwarz and Stone (2004b, p. 21).

Following Kahneman et al. (2004a) mean positive and negative affect was determined. Positive affect is the average of the happy and enjoying myself feeling categories. Negative affect is the average of frustrated/annoyed, depressed, hassled/pushed around, angry/hostile, worried/anxious and criticised/put-down feeling categories. The mean positive affect was 71, indicating that the practicum experience is, on the whole, associated with positive feelings. The mean negative affect was 19.4 indicating that although negative feeling is present, it is not overwhelming for most participants. The most strongly identified negative feeling was associated

Table 2.2 Feelings experienced during practicum (rated out of a possible 100%)

Affect	Feeling	Average rating	Standard deviation
Positive affect	Happy	71	±26.3
	Enjoying myself	71	±25.1
Other affect	Tired	65	±29.9
	Impatient for it to end	30.4	±32.2
Negative affect	Worried/anxious	43.1	±30.8
	Frustrated/annoyed	28.2	±28.1
	Depressed	14.6	±26.8
	Criticised/put-down	12.4	±29.5
	Hassled/pushed around	12.2	±28.1
	Angry/hostile	5.7	±18.7

with worry and anxiousness. Unsurprisingly, given the intensity of the practicum experience and long days associated with planning, travel and attendance, tiredness was also a feeling strongly associated with practicum participation.

Self-reported Best Things About Undertaking Practicum Placement

Prior research has found that most of the learning on placement occurs in non-theoretical areas such as time management and the development of self-confidence (Abery, Drummond, & Bevan, 2015). Respondents were asked to identify the best things about undertaking a placement. As shown in Table 2.3, exposure to the 'real world' of teaching was the most commonly reported benefit. The opportunity for professional development and to apply knowledge and skills gained in a workplace context (25%, n = 43) were also commonly reported. However, despite the rhetoric surrounding the purported employability enhancing benefits of placement (Crebert, Bates, Bell, Patrick, & Cragnolini, 2004), these did not feature prominently in pre-service teacher accounts of the best things. Instead, as shown in the following quote there was a sense that placements had the purpose of confirming the career choice of pre-service teachers:

> [by] giving an understanding of what the job entails, including relationships, politics, time management and planning. Having insight into these things help you better prepare for the 'real' world, and get a feeling for whether it is something you truly see yourself doing in the future (undergraduate).

Practicum participation was seen as having the benefit of providing the "hands-on experience" necessary "to confirm that you can do it, and importantly that you want to do it" (postgraduate). This opportunity to test skills and abilities in the context of a live classroom was considered to be important in making these judgments as "until you are in a situation where students see you as a teacher, you cannot gain

Table 2.3 Top five best things about undertaking placement	Number	Theme	Per cent (%)	n
	1	Practical 'real-world' experience	64	110
	2	Opportunity for professional development	30	52
	3	Opportunity to apply knowledge/skills	25	43
	4	Exposure to industry	17	30
	5	Opportunity to develop professional networks	8	14

the experience to determine your own abilities" (postgraduate). Given the nature of teaching as an occupation, it is surprising that very few respondents rated interactions with students as one of the best things about placement; it was only mentioned by seven (4%) respondents. Instead, practicum was primarily associated with applying the theoretical knowledge learned at university in a practical way that supports future learning and to consolidate skills across successive placements.

> Real world experience, there's nothing like it! Everything our lectures have been talking about finally makes sense now we've been teaching in a real classroom. I will have many more questions to take back to uni (postgraduate).

> As a pre-service teacher you get the opportunity to see what school life is like. You get to put all your knowledge to the test and enhance all the skills you learn throughout your degree so far. Personally I believe that I had ample opportunities to test myself and teach my own classes, this then helped me to learn and grow as a teacher (undergraduate).

Self-reported Worst Things About Undertaking Practicum Placement

Despite the learning benefits associated with practicum, some aspects of practicum are challenging for participants. As shown in Table 2.4, respondents were also asked to identify the worst thing about undertaking a placement. The most commonly identified drawback was the financial stress associated with participating in an unpaid placement (32%, n = 53). Other commonly reported downsides connected to student personal circumstances included the challenges associated with balancing work, life, and study (25%, n = 41) and the stresses associated with meeting the academic requirements of their degree (16%, n = 27). What was clear from the responses to this open-ended question was the way that multiple factors combine to impact the practicum experience (Grant-Smith et al., 2017; Macdonald, 1992). Many respondents highlighted the challenges presented by an intersection of lack of time, lack of money, lack of experience and conflict with other commitments.

> Money, attempting to fund yourself whilst working a job you have never done before and needing the time outside school hours to make resources and do assignments (undergraduate).

> Workload, hours and hours of prep and review on top of full 8 h days, is draining. It's not about being shy of hard work, it's about 12 + hour days on top of having a family, etc (postgraduate).

As might be expected, a major challenge associated with the practicum workplace was problematic interactions with supervising teachers or other staff (24%, n = 40). Respondents also identified issues associated with the structure of their placement (20%, n = 34) such as the length and block nature of placements and the total number of required placement hours. The block structure of placements has been found to have a significant impact on the ability of students to cope financially as it limits their ability to simultaneously undertake, or continue, part-time or casual work (Moore et al., 2012). This was a concern for both postgraduate and undergraduate pre-service teachers.

> Unfortunately many people, including myself, were unable to work normal jobs during placement. This was an inconvenience as I have rent and bills to pay, and it was extremely hard to go about paying my bills as I was unable to earn money (undergraduate).

> The lack of understanding from the university about the amount of stress, money, time and commitment it takes to undertake placement. It is not easy to simply ask for time off work and expect to still have a job post placement or to save enough money to be able to afford to live for the 4–6 + weeks it takes to complete without working (postgraduate).

The Financial Impacts of Practicum Participation

Students experiencing stress during practicum due to financial constraints may be a growing phenomenon (Timmins & Kaliszer, 2002). However, while it is acknowledged in the literature that students undertaking degree programmes that require practicum will incur additional financial expenses (Ralph, Walker, & Wimmer, 2009), the impact of this on the student and on their practicum experience has remained under-examined.

Students' financial circumstances and concerns about finances have the potential to impact their health and well-being as those who encounter financial difficulties may experience greater levels of stress and negative emotions which can impact their mental health (Heckman et al., 2014; Jessop et al., 2005). Andrews and Chong (2011, p. 17) found that students who indicated they were struggling financially, or who reported having adequate finances, demonstrated more psychological distress, stress, anxiety and depression than those who reported secure financial circumstances.

Financial stress may be experienced as either specific or repeated instances of financial hardship or a continuation of endemic poverty while studying (Lloyd & Turale, 2001). Respondents were asked about their subjective experience of financial stress at various times during the academic year, specifically the periods outside of the semester (n = 166), during the semester (n = 167) and during their practicum placement (n = 168). Following Andrews and Chong (2011), the subjective self-report measures of financially secure, adequate and struggling were used to determine financial security in each of these time periods. Financially secure was defined as

	Number	Theme	Per cent (%)	n
Table 2.4 Top five worst things about undertaking placement	1	Financial stress	32	53
	2	Study/work/life balance	25	41
	3	Supervising teacher/staff interactions	24	40
	4	Placement structure	20	34
	5	Academic stress	16	27

| 56%
n=93 | | | | | 41%
n=68 | | 3%
n=5 | Outside of semester |

| 25%
n=43 | | 68%
n=114 | | | 7%
n=11 | During semester |

| 13%
n=22 | 33%
n=56 | | 54%
n=90 | During placement |

Legend

☐ Financially secure ▨ Financially adequate ■ Financially struggling

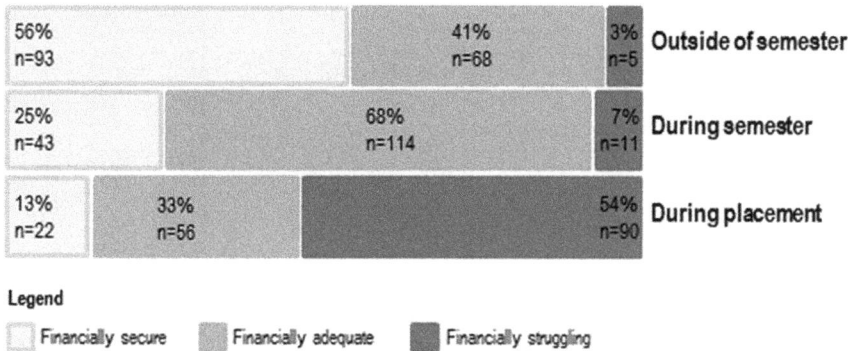

Fig. 2.2 Self-reported financial circumstances outside semester, during semester and during placement

being "able to pay for what I want", financially adequate was defined as being "able to pay for necessities but not much else" and financially struggling was defined as "struggling to pay for necessities". As shown in Fig. 2.2, financial hardship was experienced by more than half of respondents (54%, n = 90) during placement compared to only seven per cent during the academic semester when not participating in placement. Given the extended nature of education placements, this is concerning.

Significant differences were found within all three time periods: outside semester X^2 (2, n = 166) = 74.4, p = 0.01, during semester X^2 (2, n = 167) = 100.3, p = 0.01 and during placement X^2 (2, n = 168) = 41.3, p = 0.01. Significant differences were also found within the circumstance categories of secure X^2 (2, n = 157) = 51.3, p = 0.01, adequate X^2 (2, n = 238) = 23.6, p = 0.01 and struggling X^2 (2, n = 106) = 127.5, p = 0.01). Respondents reported feeling the most financially secure outside of semester (n = 93) and the least secure during placement (n = 22). During the semester, the majority of students reported having adequate financial circumstances, (n = 114) but during placement, the majority of students reported to be struggling financially. These findings illustrate the transience of financial hardship in that the majority of respondents felt more financially secure outside of the semester with their financial circumstances becoming less secure, to the point of struggling, while undertaking a placement.

Financial Stress and Hardship Experienced During Placement

The main contributor to the financial stress and hardship experienced by pre-service teachers was the loss of income (41%, n = 59) for anywhere between two and eight weeks. While this might not seem a long period in the context of a degree programme, the impact of placement on earnings was put into perspective by an undergraduate student who noted: [I] can't work for 2 weeks, which means no income

Table 2.5 Top five additional costs incurred due to placement

Number	Theme	Per cent (%)	n
1	Loss of income	41	59
2	Transport	40	57
3	Resources and materials	31	45
4	Work appropriate clothing	20	28
5	Childcare	10	14

for 2 weeks (or more as placements get longer). The "financial burden of placements" (Wray & McCall, 2007), caused by lack of income during the placement period, is exacerbated by the additional costs incurred as a direct result of participation. As shown in Table 2.5, the most common cost incurred was travel to and from placement, additional transport costs including fuel and parking, particularly if the placement site was not located conveniently to public transport routes or the timing or availability of services was not aligned with the hours worked. For some respondents, this included "having to pay tolls to minimise the extremely long drive to and from placement site" (part-time postgraduate). An undergraduate student who reported being financially secure outside of semester, financially adequate during the semester and financially struggling during placement described the financial impact of their most recent practicum experience like this:

> The placement I was allocated was in Noosa; this impacted me financially as I live in a rental property in Brisbane. Travelling up to Noosa was an additional cost I was not prepared for. Also, there was no way for me to work while I was up there as I am also employed in Brisbane. So this hindered my ability to pay rent and bills as I had no income for two weeks.

The purchase of additional resources and materials was also a significant cost for pre-service teachers, but one not necessarily experienced to the same extent by students from other disciplines (Grant-Smith et al., 2017). These additional expenses were usually the purchase of teaching supplies and materials for student use in the classroom. Purchasing "resources that the school does not have so I can get a good result" (postgraduate) was seen as a necessary expense by some respondents. These expenses, such as printing, laminating, resource making and "personal hotspot to access [the] Internet while on placement", were often incurred as they were "not offered by school" (postgraduate). These additional costs associated with the purchase of resources for activities and lessons were clearly articulated by an undergraduate student: Teachers have expressed the amount of money they spend each year to prepare their room and lessons and were not eager for pre-service teachers to use their resources.

Because uniforms or other specialist attire are not required for pre-service teachers, costs were associated with having access to a sufficient professional wardrobe. Having enough suitable outfits for the workplace was also a significant and sometimes unanticipated additional expense. This expense was exacerbated by the dress code that exists at some schools.

> I find that the level of professionalism at different schools makes it hard to always wear the same clothes from the prac before. State schools are fine with wearing jeans, whereas private you are not allowed jeans and have to dress smart-smart casual (undergraduate).
>
> The school I was placed at had a very rigorous staff clothing policy (covering arms and legs, loose) so I had to buy new clothes on top of my prior professional attire (postgraduate).

Even respondents who reported a positive practicum experience highlighted the financial challenges associated with participation: The placement itself was amazing; the only thing I could think of was the financial hardship during it—not being able to work, etc (postgraduate). These findings are generally consistent with those of Moore et al. (2012) who found the most common financial impacts associated with practicum participation included: loss of income; transport; accommodation; food; the purchase of work appropriate clothing; placement materials; and childcare.

As financial losses are incurred with each placement (Moore et al., 2012), this may have a cumulative impact over multiple placements. Respondents noted the potential impact that financial hardship can have on the practicum experience and their personal performance: "The fact that I have to take time off work and therefore don't receive any income ... is a huge financial stress which can impact my performance during placement" (undergraduate). However, there was an apparent conflict between placements that were sufficiently long to allow participants to become comfortable, competent and confident in the classroom against the financial impact of extended placements.

> The inability to work for four weeks is hard ... [but] four weeks is not enough time to establish decent relationships with the students. Because of this, you can't connect with them and it takes so long to get control and respect from the students. As a result of this, behaviour management is pretty much impossible (undergraduate).

Support Access and Awareness Among Pre-service Teachers

As reported in Table 2.6 respondents were most likely to seek support from family and friends (55%) or to seek no support at all (43%). Very low levels of access to university support were reported. As reported in Table 2.7, respondents were most aware of the availability of counselling but many chose not to access this service. There was a generally low level of awareness of most other support services available such as the food bank, work-integrated learning (WIL) bursaries and faculty equity support. The most accessed university support was equity scholarships, but these were accessed by fewer than ten per cent of respondents. This can be compared to close to half the respondents being aware of the availability of equity scholarships but being unable or ineligible to access one. One undergraduate respondent noted her disappointment in the way the university had handled her request for assistance: "I applied for uni scholarship while on prac but was told that I was not poor enough and that I could afford to eat noodles if I wanted".

Table 2.6 Support accessed while undertaking placement (n = 164)

Type of support	n	%
Support from family and friends	90	55
I did not access any support	71	43
Financial support from the university	18	11
Other support from the university	21	13
Other support	21	13

Table 2.7 Awareness and use of university support services

	Support awareness and access							
	I was aware of but could not access this support		I was aware of but chose not to access this support		I was aware of and accessed this support		I was unaware of the availability of this support	
Type of Support[a]	N	%	N	%	N	%	N	%
Food bank	28	21	41	30	1	1	64	48
Counselling services	13	9	92	66	7	5	28	20
Welfare officers	20	15	45	34	2	1	66	50
Equity scholarships	69	49	30	21	9	6	33	24
WIL bursaries	39	29	23	17	3	2	70	52
Faculty equity support	23	17	22	16	2	2	88	65

[a]The *foodbank* is run by the student guild and provides access to basic food items. A *work-integrated learning (WIL) bursary* is a payment for students undertaking a placement and experiencing financial hardship. Eligibility is determined through an appointment with student counselling services and supporting documentation provided by the student. Low-income students experiencing financial hardship can apply for an *equity scholarship* to assist with covering the costs of living and studying more generally

As reported in Table 2.8, the main reason respondents gave for choosing not to access university support services they were aware of is that they were not required. Being ineligible to apply was the main reason given for being unable to access university support services that they were aware of. Altruism, based on a belief that there were other students with greater need, also featured prominently in choices not to access available support.

Table 2.8 Reasons for not accessing university support services (n = 108)

	Support awareness and access			
	I was aware of but could not access support (n = 69)		I was aware but chose not to access support (n = 108)	
Reason	N	%	N	%
Support not required	5	7	61	57
Eligibility	58	84	18	17
Too busy to access support	6	9	18	17
Altruism	3	4	15	14
Accessibility of support	3	4	11	10
Accessed other support	1	1	8	7
Difficulty asking for help/charity/pride	–	–	5	5

Supporting the Pre-service Teacher

Pre-service teachers are seeking greater levels of pastoral care, staff support and empathy from universities and their university supervisors (Smith & Lev-Ari, 2005). The university-based supervisors tasked with supporting pre-service teachers while undertaking their practicum, often straddle the multiple roles of imparting necessary theoretical knowledge (Smith & Lev-Ari, 2005), developing and maintaining positive and productive partnerships with the schools and responding to the needs pre-service teachers as required, while maintaining a 'weak position' overall in the context of the teaching practicum (Wilkens et al., 2015). Despite the prevalence of stress and anxiety among students, staff are often unaware of the extent of the personal and financial difficulties students experience (Creedon, 2015). This lack of knowledge, combined with their own work-related pressures, may result in a "lack of empathy from lecturers about practicum pressures" (postgraduate, part-time) or a superficial engagement with students on practicum.

> I've attempted to contact my university supervisor who has not even had the professional decency to acknowledge my email or confirm my contact. There has been very little communication regarding placements (postgraduate, part-time).
>
> In this placement (just like the previous two) ... it really does feel like you are going it alone. Funnily enough, the odd email from our supervisor asking us whether everything is going ok doesn't actually achieve anything at all. If this university was serious about this sort of thing, they would provide some sort of supervisor who at least visits my class and observes at least one lesson (undergraduate).

While it is recognised that implementation may prove to be challenging, a number of low cost but potentially high impact initiatives were proposed by respondents. These included providing an "online tutorial or tutor to answer simplistic questions regarding lesson planning, topic content, ACARA[2] documents, etc." while on practicum, providing a "seminar on the different types of help available for placement time", and improved processes for dealing with difficulties experienced during placement.

While it is very unlikely that universities will be able to provide students with the financial assistance they desire, students should be advised of the 'true' costs of their degree, including placements, as unexpected expenditures can throw students financially off balance (Creedon, 2015). Improved processes could also be put in place to support university placement officers to address issues associated with practicum, such as minimising the travel burden experienced by some students.

> Before placing students, survey them on their considerations such as transport. Four hours of commute a day for field experience is ridiculous and has impacted my health and wellbeing (undergraduate, part-time).

Johnstone et al. (2016, p. 481) argue that the financial hardship experienced by students undertaking placement "should not be regarded as a problem for students to endure and manage". Instead, they argue that collaborative effort among multiple stakeholders is required. A financial anxiety scale (Archuleta, Dale, & Spann, 2013) could be used to identify students who are experiencing increased levels of financial distress to target those who require assistance or referral to an appropriate professional.

Deasy et al. (2014) argue that in order to properly equip students for practicum, educators should ensure that programmes of study that include a practicum component also offer opportunities to learn coping strategies, life skills and stress management. A part-time postgraduate respondent proposed providing "opportunities for new students to hear from experienced students first-hand what actually happens in placements. That way they can be more aware of what to expect and how to prepare". Workshops could be provided for the most common stressors encountered by students (Ross et al., 1999), which given our findings indicate practicum students would benefit from personal finance training in addition to emotional, institutional and academic supports. Such an initiative could provide the opportunity for students to learn from financial counsellors and "recent graduates who have 'survived' or 'thrived' through their poverty experiences" (Lloyd & Turale, 2001, p. 13).

Goetz, Cude, Nielsen, Chatterjee, and Mimura's (2011) research confirmed student interest in personal financial education through a combination of online resources, workshops and financial counselling. Improving students' financial efficacy and confidence through such initiatives could help students better respond to financial stressors (Heckman et al., 2014) as there is a positive relationship between higher levels of financial knowledge and reduced financial stress (Britt, Mendiola, Schink, Tibbetts, & Jones, 2016). To effectively support students, financial

---

[2]Australian Curriculum Assessment and Reporting Authority.

knowledge should be offered in addition to financial support (Britt et al., 2016) as improving students' financial literacy can equip them with the skills to manage the financial impact of practicum, leading to less financial stress and improved well-being. This may need to be offered more than once as many students experience financial hardships during placement but do not always expect finances to be a concern at the beginning of their degree (Wray & McCall, 2007).

Finally, some respondents propose that universities and registration/accreditation bodies may need to be more flexible and consider the potential for structural changes to placement requirements. An example was the suggestion that "placement should be offered part-time to enable students who are suffering due to health concerns, financial concerns, etc" (postgraduate, part-time). Students are not always aware of constraints experienced by the university in organising placements. For example, a part-time undergraduate respondent proposed the currently unviable possibility of students completing "two subjects that require … field experience at once" to reduce the total number of placements needed in the degree programme, which if implemented, could result in a lack of adherence with accreditation standards which set a mandated number of days of placement. However, it does raise the possibility of reimagining how professional experience is embedded within initial teacher education programmes to potentially move away from predominantly block placements to a more integrated approach, which could relieve some of the financial strain associated with practicum participation.

Conclusions and Future Directions

Students are overwhelming in their appraisal of practicum as a valuable 'real-world' learning experience. However, as the respondent quote used as the title of the chapter shows participation is not without costs. This chapter does not question the potentially transformative impact that professional experience opportunities can have on participants, nor do we dispute that practicum participation has pedagogical value. Rather we advocate that the zeal for placements is tempered by an explicit recognition of the costs of participation and the unintended impact these can have on students' performance during placement. The financial implications of practicum have not always been an issue as in the past students were paid during placement (Timmins & Kaliszer, 2002). Given that this is no longer the case, we concur with Schofield et al. (2009, p. 134) that "there are significant risks in a system that exposes students to a reduction in earnings that support their capacity to study".

The introduction of non-academic entry requirements for admission to an initial teacher education course provides an additional unknown moving forward (Louden, 2015). While having the potential to increase the quality of entrants and graduates by understanding their interests and motivation for wanting to enter the profession, it also introduces an additional hurdle that may exclude certain students with, for example literacy and communication difficulties. It is yet to be seen how these new entry requirements may impact the identified stressors and challenges associated with professional experience as highlighted by pre-service teachers and is something that warrants ongoing investigation.

Moore et al. (2012, p. 211) believe that "more needs to be done to raise concern across the [higher education] sector about the cost of WIL to students". It is imperative that all stakeholders involved in managing, administering and promoting practicum be cognisant of the potential impacts on participants and act to reduce those where possible. It is critical that the financial impacts of practicum participation do not restrict participation and that the impacts on participation are reduced where possible. This is important for safeguarding the well-being of the student but also to ensure that they enter the teaching profession with a positive outlook. This was succinctly expressed by an undergraduate respondent who noted: "While bad experiences are just as valuable as the good ones, it can make you lose passion before you even begin your career".

References

Abery, E., Drummond, C., & Bevan, N. (2015). Work integrated learning: What do the students want? A qualitative study of health sciences students' experiences of a non-competency based placement. *Student Success, 6*(2), 87–91.

Andrews, A., & Chong, J. L. (2011). Exploring the wellbeing of students studying at an Australian university. *Journal of the Australian & New Zealand Student Services Association, 37,* 9–38.

Archuleta, K. L., Dale, A., & Spann, S. M. (2013). College students and financial distress: Exploring debt, financial satisfaction, and financial anxiety. *Journal of Financial Counseling & Planning, 24*(2), 50–62.

Beck, C., & Kosnick, C. (2002). Components of a good practicum placement: Student teacher perceptions. *Teacher Education Quarterly, 29*(2), 91–98.

Britt, S. L., Mendiola, M. R., Schink, G. H., Tibbetts, R. H., & Jones, S. H. (2016). Financial stress, coping strategy, and academic achievement of college students. *Journal of Financial Counseling & Planning, 27*(2), 172–183.

Bryman, A. (2008). *Social research methods* (3rd ed.). New York: Oxford University Press.

Crebert, G., Bates, M., Bell, B., Patrick, C. J., & Cragnolini, V. (2004). Developing generic skills at university, during work placement and in employment: Graduates' perceptions. *Higher Education Research & Development, 23*(2), 147–165.

Creedon, D. (2015). The experience of financial hardship on mature students' social and academic integration. *International Journal for Cross-Disciplinary Subjects in Education, 5*(2), 2471–2481.

Danyluk, P. (2013). The role of the pre-practicum in lessening student teacher stress: Student teachers' perceptions of stress during practicum. *Action in Teacher Education, 35*(5–6), 323–334.

Deasy, C., Coughlan, B., Pironom, J., Jourdan, D., & Mannis-McNamara, P. (2014). Psychological distress and coping amongst higher education students: A mixed method enquiry. *PLoS One, 9*(12). https://doi.org/10.1371/journal.pone.0115193.

Fosnacht, K., & Calderone, S. M. (2017). Undergraduate financial stress, financial self-efficacy, and major choice: A multi-institutional study. *Journal of Financial Therapy, 8*(1), 107–123.

Giannakaki, M.-S., Hobson, A. J., & Malderez, A. (2011). Student teachers' perceptions of the effectiveness of their initial preparation. *European Journal of Education Research, Development & Policy, 46*(4), 456–473.

Goetz, J., Cude, B. J., Nielsen, R. B., Chatterjee, S., & Mimura, Y. (2011). College-based personal finance education: Student interest in three delivery methods. *Journal of Financial Counseling & Planning, 22*(1), 27–42.

Grant-Smith, D., & Gillett-Swan, J. (2017). Managing the personal impacts of practicum: Examining the experiences of graduate diploma in education students. In J. Nuttall, A. Kostogriz, M. Jones, & J. Martin (Eds.), *Teacher education policy & practice: Evidence of impact, impact of evidence* (pp. 97–112). Singapore: Springer.

Grant-Smith, D., Gillett-Swan, J., & Chapman. R. (2017). *WiL wellbeing: Exploring the impacts of unpaid practicum on student wellbeing.* Perth: National Centre for Student Equity in Higher Education. https://www.ncsehe.edu.au/wp-content/uploads/2017/07/GrantSmith_WIL.pdf.

Grudnoff, L. (2011). Rethinking the practicum: Limitations and possibilities. *Asia-Pacific Journal of Teacher Education, 39*(3), 223–234.

Harding, J. (2011). Financial circumstances, financial difficulties and academic achievement among first-year undergraduates. *Journal of Further & Higher Education, 35*(4), 483–499.

Heckman, S., Lim, H., & Monalto, C. (2014). Factors related to financial stress among college students. *Journal of Financial Therapy, 5*(1), 19–39.

Jessop, D. C., Herberts, C., & Solomon, L. (2005). The impact of financial circumstances on student health. *British Journal of Health Psychology, 10*(3), 421–439.

Johnstone, E., Brough, M., Crane, P., Marston, G., & Correa-Velez, I. (2016). Field placement and the impact of financial stress on social work and human service students. *Australian Social Work, 69*(4), 481–494.

Joo, S., Durband, D. B., & Grable, J. (2008). The academic impact of financial stress on college students. *Journal of College Student Retention: Research, Theory & Practice, 10*(3), 287–305.

Kahneman, D., Krueger, A. B., Schkade, D. A., Schwarz, N., & Stone, A. A. (2004a). The survey method for characterizing daily life experience: The day reconstruction method. *Science, 306*(5702), 1176–1780.

Kahneman, D., Krueger, A. B., Schkade, D. A., Schwarz, N., & Stone, A. A. (2004b) *The day reconstruction method (DRM): Instrumentation documentation.* https://dornsife.usc.edu/assets/sites/780/docs/drm_documentation_july_2004.pdf.

Kanno, H., & Koesk, G. F. (2010). MSW students' satisfaction with their field placement: The role of preparedness and supervision quality. *Journal of Social Work Education, 46*(1), 23–38.

Krauss, S. E. (2005). Research paradigms and meaning making: A primer. *The Qualitative Report, 10*(4), 758–770.

Krueger, A. B., & Schkade, D. A. (2007). The reliability of subjective well-being measures. *Journal of Public Economics, 92*(8–9), 1833–1845.

Lawson, T., Cakmak, M., Gunduz, M., & Busher, H. (2015). Research on teaching practicum: A systematic review. *European Journal of Teacher Education, 38*(3), 392–407.

Le Cornu, R., & Ewing, R. (2008). Reconceptualising professional experiences in pre-service teacher education: Reconstructing the past to embrace the future. *Teaching & Teacher Education, 24*(7), 1799–1812.

Lloyd, D., & Turale, S. (2001). New conceptions of student neediness and directions for better responses. In *Australian Association for Research in Education Conference.* December 2–6, 2001, Fremantle.

Louden, W. (2015). *Standardised assessment of initial teacher education: Environmental scan and case studies.* Australian Insitute for Teaching and School Leadership: Melbourne.

Macdonald, C. J. (1992). The multiplicity of factors creating stress during the teaching practicum: The student-teachers' perspective. *Project Innovation, 113,* 48–58.

Moore, K., Ferns, S., & Peach, D. (2012). The ACEN student scholarships: A profile of financial hardship and work integrated learning. In *Proceedings of the Australian Collaborative Education Network National Conference* (pp. 201–212). Geelong: Deakin University.

OECD. (2014). *Teaching and learning international survey [TALIS] 2013 results: An international perspective in teaching and learning.* Paris: OECD Publishing.

Ralph, E., Walker, K., & Wimmer, R. (2009). Practicum and clinical experiences: Postpracticum students' views. *Journal of Nursing Education, 48*(8), 434–440.

Ross, S. E., Niebling, B. C., & Heckert, T. M. (1999). Sources of stress among college students. *College Student Journal, 33*(2), 312–317.

Schofield, D., Keane, S., Fletcher, S., Shrestha, R., & Percival, R. (2009). Loss of income and levels of scholarship support for students on rural clinical placements: A survey of medical, nursing and allied health students. *Australian Journal of Rural Health, 17*(3), 134–140.

Smith, K., & Lev-Ari, L. (2005). The place of the practicum in pre-service teacher education: The voice of students. *Asia-Pacific Journal of Teacher Education, 33*(3), 289–302.

Spooner-Lane, R., Tangen, D., & Campbell, M. (2007). When your first year is your final year: Changing perceptions of practicum through NESB pre-service teachers' eyes. In *First Year of Higher Education Conference*. July 6, 2007, Brisbane.

Teacher Education Ministerial Advisory Group [TEMAG]. (2014). *Action now: Classroom ready teachers*. Report available via http://www.studentsfirst.gov.au/teacher-education-ministerial-advisory-group.

Timmins, F., & Kaliszer, M. (2002). Aspects of nurse education programmes that frequently cause stress to nursing students: Fact-finding sample survey. *Nurse Education Today, 22*(3), 203–211.

Watson, S. J., Barber, B. L., & Dziurawiec, S. (2015). The role of economizing and financial strain in Australian university students' psychological well-being. *Journal of Family Economic Issues, 36*, 421–433.

Wilkens, C. P., Ashton, J. R., Maurer, D. M., & Smith, S. (2015). Some of this is not your fault: Imperfect placements, student teachers, and university supervision. *Schools: Studies in Education, 12*(2), 329–341.

Wray, N., & McCall, L. (2007). Money matters: Students' perceptions of the costs associated with placements. *Medical Education, 41*(10), 975–981.

Author Biographies

Deanna Grant-Smith is a Senior Lecturer at the QUT Business School where she researches youth employment and employability, work-integrated learning and the education-to-employment transitions of disadvantaged job seekers and early career professionals across a range of disciplines including business, education, nursing, and urban and regional planning. In particular, she has explored the challenges and potential for exploitation associated with unpaid work and internships. This research has been published in a wide range of journals including *Journal of Youth Studies, Australian Universities' Review, International Journal of Management Reviews* and *Sociology*. She was jointly named the 2016 Australian and New Zealand Academy of Management (ANZAM) Early Career Researcher and in 2017 received an Australian Awards for Universities Teaching Citation for Outstanding Contributions to Student Learning. She is a Senior Fellow of the Higher Education Academy and Member of the QUT Work/Industry Futures Research Program, leading its Employability and Learning sub-theme.

Laura de Zwaan is a Lecturer in Accountancy at the QUT Business School. While her primary research area is superannuation, she also has a strong research and pedagogical interest in personal finance and financial literacy of university students. She has published her research on financial literacy and education in a range of journals including *Journal of Australasian Tax Teachers Association, Financial Planning Research Journal* and *Australian Accounting Review*. She is a Member of the Financial Planning Academic Forum and was elected to the QUT UniSuper Consultative Committee for a 4-year term commencing May 2017.

Renee Chapman is a Senior Research Assistant at the QUT Business School and the QUT Faculty of Education working across a range of projects associated with executive education, student equity in higher education, and unpaid clinical and initial teacher education field placements. She is experienced in undertaking a range of qualitative and quantitative research approaches and specialises in mixed methods research. Her research approach is underpinned by a strong commitment to methodological rigour and ensuring that participant's voice is central to research accounts. She is also a professional photographer.

Jenna Gillett-Swan is a Senior Lecturer in the QUT Faculty of Education. Her research focuses on well-being, rights, voice and participation. She also specialises in qualitative child-centred participatory research methodologies and has investigated different aspects of how well-being is conceptualised and defined by students. She is a Senior Fellow of the Higher Education Academy and received the 2016 Australia Teacher Education Association (ATEA) Research Recognition Award for Early Career Researchers. She is the co-editor of *Children's Rights, Educational Research and the UNCRC* (Symposium Books). She has also published in a range of journals including *Qualitative Research*, *Educational Research*, *Journal of Learning Design*, *Children & Society* and the *European Educational Research Journal*. She guest-edited the *Global Studies of Childhood journal* special issue on *Children's Rights in a 21st Century Digital World* (2016) and with Deanna Grant-Smith was guest editor of the *Asia Pacific Journal of Teacher Education* special issue on recognising and responding to the factors influencing diverse pre-service teacher experiences of practicum (2017).

Chapter 3
Teacher Education for an Uncertain Future: Implications of PISA's Global Competence

Donella J. Cobb and Daniel Couch

Abstract In 2018, the Organisation for Economic Cooperation and Development's (OECD) is set to introduce an assessment of Global Competence in its Programme for International Student Achievement (PISA). This assessment lays the foundation for a set of knowledge, skills, values and beliefs that the OECD considers necessary to become a globally competent citizen. Throughout this chapter, we identify and critique the intended socialising function of PISA's Global Competence and consider its implications for Initial Teacher Education (ITE). We do this by drawing on Bernstein's theoretical tools to engage in a critical analysis of PISA's Global Competence framework. Our analysis reveals three key findings: (1) PISA's Global Competence acts as a symbolic regulator of consciousness, (2) PISA's Global Competence facilitates a new form of global pedagogic governance and (3) ITE can play an important role in either reproducing, disrupting or transforming the socialising function of PISA's Global Competence. In conclusion, we argue that engaging with Comparative and International Education scholarship will prepare pre-service teachers to respond to the complexities and demands of an uncertain educational future within an increasingly globalised educational landscape.

Keywords PISA · Global competence · Bernstein · Initial teacher education Comparative and International Education

D. J. Cobb (✉)
The University of Waikato, Hamilton, New Zealand
e-mail: donella.cobb@waikato.ac.nz

D. Couch
The University of Auckland, Auckland, New Zealand
e-mail: d.couch@auckland.ac.nz

© Springer Nature Singapore Pte Ltd. 2018
D. Heck and A. Ambrosetti (eds.), *Teacher Education In and For Uncertain Times*,
https://doi.org/10.1007/978-981-10-8648-9_3

Introduction

It might be said that the only certainty in the future of education is its uncertainty. There is, however, a case to be made for a further certainty; that with growing frequency and speed, local education ideas, policies and practices will be increasingly determined by responses to global events, debates and agendas (Robertson, 2016). Education policy is increasingly being influenced or determined by events and policy groups that operate on an international level (Volante & Fazio, 2018). This is not a new phenomenon. However, the intensity of this interconnectedness and the growth of pathways for education ideas to travel between global and local leads to a rising uncertainty for the future of education. This chapter raises critical awareness to the socialising function of Programme for International Student Achievement's (PISA) Global Competence and considers the implications for Initial Teacher Education (ITE).

In 2016, the Organisation for Economic Cooperation and Development (OECD) signalled its proposal to include Global Competence in its 2018 PISA measurement. Defined as the ability to "mobilise knowledge, skills, attitudes and values" (OECD, 2016, p. 2), this assessment of Global Competence intends to prepare students "to engage with and act in the world" (p. 2). The OECD defines Global Competence as the:

> capacity to analyse global and intercultural issues critically and from multiple perspectives, to understand how differences affect perceptions, judgements, and ideas of self and others, and to engage in open, appropriate and effective interactions with others from different backgrounds on the basis of a shared respect for human dignity. (OECD, 2016, p. 4)

Fifteen-year-olds in approximately 80 countries will be tested on their knowledge, skills, values and attitudes towards global competence, including their knowledge of global issues, their ability to speak more than one language and the demonstration of their attitudes towards cultural diversity. Evidence from this assessment is intended to provide governments with data to reform education policy, curriculum development and teacher education programmes (OECD, 2016). Teacher education and professional training are considered central to the implementation of Global Competence, and the OECD argues that there is a critical need for Initial Teacher Education (ITE) to "address and support teachers' global competence development" (OECD, 2016, p. 19). However, this radical move to reform education based on an assessment of globally regulated values, attitudes, skills and knowledge brings considerable uncertainty, particularly for teacher education. What does this mean for the future of teacher education? How can educators, academics and ITE providers best prepare pre-service teachers for this increasingly uncertain future?

In this chapter, we examine the OECD's *Global competency for an inclusive world* (OECD, 2016) framework. The framework outlines the introduction of Global Competence into PISA's upcoming 2018 assessment. The chapter begins with an overview of critical policy scholarship on the OECD and PISA. We then draw on Bernstein's theoretical tools, from a critical realist position, to argue that PISA's Global Competence operates as a symbolic regulator of consciousness to shape a new form of pedagogic identity that serves the interests of a global marketplace. We demonstrate how ITE plays an important role in this identity reconstruction by either reproducing or disrupting these new pedagogic identities. We conclude by stating that stronger engagement with the field of Comparative and International Education (CIE) will prepare pre-service teachers for uncertain futures within an increasingly globalised educational landscape.

The OECD's Education Agenda

The origins of the OECD and PISA are well chronicled. It is not our intent to replicate that historiography. However, it is important to understand the organisational intent of the OECD to examine the ideation of PISA's Global Competence. To this end, we briefly explore literature from critical policy scholarship on the OECD and PISA. The OECD's convention of 1961 sets out its purpose as "promoting sustainable economic growth and development, maximising employment and living standards, and nurturing the global trading regime" (Woodward, 2009, p. 4). Members' states come from 35 of the most advanced national economies in the world, although, in recent times, this has extended to emerging economies such as Mexico, Chile and Turkey. The organisation is multifaceted, operating simultaneously as a "geographic entity, an organisational structure, a policy-making forum, a network of policy-makers, researchers and consultants, and a sphere of influence" (Henry, Lingard, Rizvi, & Taylor, 2001, p. 7). The OECD operates solely within the realm of ideas, which leads it to occupy a particular realm of influence in setting the current global education agenda (Sellar & Lingard, 2014). While education had always had an inferred role within the organisation, this became explicit during the 1990s (Lingard & Sellar, 2016).

Since its inception, the OECD's interest in education has always been framed by economic concerns (Lingard & Sellar, 2016). A key justification for the explicit policy focus on education during the late 1990s was driven by a wide subscription to human capital theory and the global emergence of a knowledge economy. Within human capital theory, education plays an instrumental economic role as it develops the individuals who constitute "a highly skilled and flexible workforce [essential] to national success within the new global knowledge economy" (Henry et al., 2001, p. 30). This saw a shift away from perceiving education's primary benefit as collective (public good) and towards the individual (private good). The knowledge economy regarded education "as the policy key to the future prosperity of nations" (Henry et al., 2001, p. 30), and this drove OECD member states to call for education data that could be internationally comparative "as surrogate measures of the potential global competitiveness of national economies" (Sellar & Lingard, 2014, p. 918). The OECD duly began to develop tools to gather and compare educational attainment (Lingard & Sellar, 2016; Volante & Fazio, 2018). The Programme for International Student Assessment was the result.

PISA international assessments take place every three years to assess the skills and knowledge of 15-year-olds in member and non-member countries who volunteer to take part. Using a subject-based cycle, PISA measures literacy, mathematics and science once every three years with the aim of creating an "internationally comparative evidence base for educational policy development and implementation" (Wiseman, 2013, p. 304). Fourty-three countries were involved in the first PISA assessment; however, by 2015 over half a million students, who were representative of 29 million 15-year-olds, were assessed in 72 countries (OECD, 2017). Generating such a significant amount of data, PISA "is one of the largest non-experimental research exercises the world has ever seen" (Murphy, 2014, p. 898). With big data comes with big influence. PISA has enabled the OECD to position itself as a primary influencer within the global education agenda. Many authors point to PISA as a key mechanism of global educational governance, in which OECD member countries leverage their position within the organisation to effectively direct national-level education reforms in member and non-member states alike (Lingard & Lewis, 2017; Volante & Fazio, 2018). Nations have used PISA's international comparisons to identify their educational problems and have responded by reforming their education systems and policies in an attempt to "move up" the rankings (Meyer & Benavot, 2013; Wiseman, 2013). This has further legitimised the role of international organisations to examine and dissect successful school systems with the aim of implementing internationally standardised curricula, pedagogy and ITE programmes as a panacea for failing education systems (Münch 2014).

It is clear from this review of literature that PISA influences national forms of education delivery. This positions teacher education within a rapidly changing and uncertain landscape, which encourages national education institutions to increasingly align and conform with PISA structures (Münch, 2014). Ultimately, this has the potential to rob local institutions, such as ITE providers, of their legitimacy and keep them "in a state of uncertainty for decades" (Münch, 2014, p. 13). This state of uncertainty for teacher education is even more imminent with the OECD's recent proposal to include the assessment of Global Competence in the 2018 PISA (OECD, 2016). Below, we analyse the *Global competency for an inclusive world* (OECD, 2016) to identify the potential implications of PISA's Global Competence on national ITE programmes.

A Bernsteinian Analysis of PISA's Global Competence

In recent years, there has been a growing interest in "putting Bernstein's theories to work" (Robertson & Sorensen, 2017, p. 3) to theorise global processes and global governance (Singh, 2015, 2017; Tyler, 2010). The explanatory power of both Bernstein's theoretical tools and his notion of a Totally Pedagogised Society (TPS) have been particularly useful for examining global policies and global governance. In his later work, Bernstein hypothesised that a market-oriented ideology would shape new forms of pedagogic identity to serve the interests of the marketplace (Bernstein, 2001). He used the term TPS to vaticinate an emerging society that he believed would shape and sustain social order by embedding discursive principles of pedagogy throughout the fabric of social life. It is through the internal shaping of consciousness, aspirations, desires and conduct that governments would gain symbolic control of the pedagogic space. Bernstein predicted that this space would socialise actors to serve the rapidly changing labour needs of a global marketplace. Of late, a growing number of scholars have extrapolated Bernstein's thesis beyond the boundaries of the nation state to examine how supranational organisations, such as the OECD, have used pedagogic tools to gain symbolic control over regional and global pedagogic spaces (see Robertson & Sorensen, 2017; Tyler, 2010). In doing so, these scholars add weight to Bernstein's vatication that a TPS would see symbolic power transform education from being a reproducer of society, to becoming a shaper of consciousness.

What makes Bernstein's work particularly relevant to our examination of PISA's Global Competence is the way he also developed a conceptual grammar to address the relationship between actors and agencies in both the transmission and acquisition of knowledge, and the production and regulation of consciousness and disposition (Bernstein, 2001). He sought to understand the social significance of these pedagogical relationships and the way that they shape cultural production, reproduction and disruption. This engagement with multiple actors and agencies is particularly useful when examining the pedagogical significance of a tool such as PISA's Global Competence. Actors and agencies can operate as agents of this symbolic control by performing various roles and functions. Bernstein (2001) defines symbolic control as "the means where consciousness, dispositions and desire are shaped and distributed through forms of communication which relay and legitimate a distribution of power and cultural categories" (p. 23). He views this field of symbolic control as a division of labour, which he suggests is divided into "specialised discourses, agents and agencies" (p. 23). For example, Bernstein maintains that teachers and schools fulfil a reproductive function while academics and institutions, such as ITE providers, can play either a reproductive role by reproducing the ideas and practices produced by governments or a transformative role by disrupting oppressive ideologies and shaping new ideas and knowledge. We return to this point later in this chapter in our analysis of PISA's Global Competence.

Bernstein (2000) maintains that biases are embedded within educational transmission. He sets out the notion of a "pedagogic device" to describe the mechanisms which relay biases and ideological messages. Pedagogic devices provide a valuable way to understand how the process of producing, transmitting and acquiring knowledge shapes and reshapes pedagogic identities. The pedagogic device, therefore, has a dual role: to act as a symbolic regulator of consciousness while also facilitating the production, reproduction and transformation of culture. Ideologies are constructed as a result of changing values in education systems. Bernstein prompts us to question the agenda behind educational changes by asking "which group is responsible for initiating the change?" (2000, p. 15), and whether such change is initiated by a dominant or a dominated group. These questions encourage us to consider why the OECD is interested in assessing certain knowledge, values and beliefs, and whose interests this information serves. An analysis of these biases is necessary to understand the social significance of this educational transmission. Bernstein (2000) identifies three rules to analyse these biases and ideological messages within this pedagogic device: the *distributive rule*, the *recontextualising rule* and the *evaluative rule*.

The distributive rule refers to the way in which a phenomenon becomes legitimised. This occurs in the abstract; something that was not previously thought *is* thought and thus becomes possible to know. Bernstein (2000) argues that this distributive rule creates, produces and distributes pedagogic discourse to privilege the dominant social group. In the case of the OECD's framework, the idea that all people can possess universal skills, values, attitudes and knowledge independent from local cultural practices is legitimated through the establishment of PISA's Global Competence assessment. This universal individual is set out and justified by OECD's Chief of Staff Ramos in her introductory comments to the framework:

> Against a context in which we all have much to gain from growing openness and connectivity, and much to lose from rising inequalities and radicalism, citizens need not only the skills to be competitive and ready for a new world of work, but more importantly they also need to develop the capacity to analyse and understand global and intercultural issues. (OECD, 2016, p. ii)

Ramos presents global competency as the answer to rising inequalities and radicalism around the world, stating that "global competencies [are] vital for individuals to thrive in a rapidly changing world and for societies to progress without leaving anyone behind" (OECD, 2016, p. ii). At this first level of analysis, we begin to see how PISA's global competence assessment lays a foundation for legitimising universal attributes and enables the OECD to gain symbolic control of the global pedagogic space.

Bernstein's notion of recontextualisation considers how ideas, such as global competence, take on new meaning as they are transmitted between actors and contexts. During this transmission, a new form of the original idea takes shape. This could be understood in terms of a Trojan Horse, whereby a seemingly innocuous or even positive notion obfuscates an alternative intent. Herein lies the crux of our argument, as we make the case that recontextualisation occurs within the ideation of Global Competence. The framework clearly identifies certain values, attitudes and skills that the OECD believes should be possessed by all. In this initial construction of the idea, several positive and desirable attributes are presented. These include attitudes of openness towards people, respect for cultural otherness, global mindedness and responsibility. It also includes the ability to interact respectfully, with empathy and flexibility (OECD, 2016, p. 13). Also, it maintains that individuals should have the ability to speak another language. However, a thematic analysis of the framework illustrates the underpinning dominance of human capital theory. It makes the case that "both employers and policy-makers... need an evidence-based approach to teaching and assessing global competence" (p. 3). Certain skills, values and behaviours are privileged to meet employers' needs within a global marketplace. In this way, the original concept of Global Competence is recontextualised from meeting largely social goals to advance a neoliberal agenda across national education curricula and ITE programmes.

Finally, the evaluative rule ensures that knowledge, skills, values and attitudes are both taught *and* acquired. Bernstein (2000) explains that the *evaluative rule* is responsible for regulating the "what" and "how" of teaching by setting standards, legitimating content, determining the form of transmission and regulating the way that knowledge is distributed to different groups in different contexts. Within the Global Competence framework, a particular emphasis is placed on pedagogic interaction. This suggests that teachers will need to "act as facilitators in activities" (OECD, 2016, p. 18) to aid the development of Global Competence, and that learner-centred pedagogy is an "innovative teaching and learning method" (p. 18) that should be supported by "the official curriculum and education authorities" (p. 19). This explicit focus on pedagogy is intended to ensure that students gain the acquisition of the skills, attitudes, values and knowledge set out by the OECD in their ideation of the globally competent individual. In the light of the identified foundation of human capital theory, the evaluative rule in this context facilitates the socialisation of students to think, behave and act in certain ways that serve the interests of a globalised labour market.

The "PISA Effect" and Teacher Education

This analysis of PISA's Global Competence framework reveals three key findings. Firstly, by understanding PISA's Global Competence as a pedagogic device, its capacity to act as a symbolic regulator of consciousness is uncovered. Our analysis of the Global Competence framework has identified an underlying intent within the notion of Global Competence which orients education further towards market interests. Labaree (2014) claims that a certain type of worker is needed to grow market economies. This has seen the OECD engineer the development of cognitive skills that are considered necessary for workers in a global marketplace (Labaree, 2014). PISA performs a crucial function in the development of this human capital production by not only establishing the criteria for the globalisation of certain skills but providing a "measure of human capital flows into economies" (Sellar & Lingard, 2013, p. 193). This has shifted the focus of assessment from understanding what people know or what people can do, to quantifying "who people are and who they could become" (Sellar & Lingard, 2013, p. 196). Münch (2014) suggests that this refocused emphasis on human capital production keeps local institutions such as schools and ITE providers in an ongoing state of uncertainty. This presents an opportunity to subtly erode and deconstruct their foundations to conform with PISA's subscription to human capital theory. By understanding PISA's Global Competence as a pedagogic device, we can see how the framework intends to reshape pedagogic identities by socialising the skills, values, behaviours and dispositions that advance human capital production.

Our second finding builds on this conceptualisation of PISA's Global Competence as a pedagogic device and proposes that PISA's Global Competence contributes to a new form of global pedagogic governance. The OECD signals that data gathered from the PISA Global Competence assessment is intended to drive national curricula reform (OECD, 2016, p. 12). This increasing control over the "what" and "how" of learning and teaching at all levels of education suggests that the OECD is positioned to gain increasing governance of the global pedagogic space. Bernstein (2001) raised concern that governance would be increasingly obtained by pedagogic means in order to serve market interests. Our analysis of PISA's Global Competence framework points to such concerns. Pykett (2009) refers to the way in which pedagogic governance is outworked through developing competencies "in every area of life" (p. 108) rather than regulating actors by external rules or direct instruction. As previously demonstrated PISA's Global Competence appears to fulfil this function by reshaping consciousness, dispositions and desires to address the needs of the market. Thus, this reorienting of pedagogic identity now seems to align with the OECD's core function; that is, to grow market economies (Tröhler, Meyer, Labaree, & Hutt, 2014). This positions the OECD to better gain symbolic control of the global pedagogic space, increasing the OECD's power to govern global education reform through indirect means.

This increasing alignment between pedagogic governance and social control is what Bernstein (2001) referred to as a Totally Pedagogised Society (TPS). Singh (2015) reminds us that a TPS creates new regimes of power by establishing new ways to communicate social control (Singh, 2015). PISA's Global Competence appears to provide an important symbolic tool to establish these new routines of introspection and regimes of power and social control. Bernstein predicted that a move towards a TPS would reposition education away from being a reproducer of society and towards playing a leading role in establishing and legitimating society. Our first finding illustrates how the framework is significant in reorienting education to become a shaper of consciousness, uncovering a new mode of regulation, governance and social control in the process (Singh, 2017). However, Bernstein's concern with such reorientation moves beyond simply determining modes of power and control. Rather, he argues that such understanding must lead to consideration of how social inequalities are reproduced, resisted, disrupted and transformed "through these new modes and networks of pedagogic communication" (Singh, 2015, p. 365). To respond to these concerns, our final finding briefly examines the agents and agencies of symbolic control.

Our third key finding demonstrates how ITE plays an important role in either reproducing or disrupting and transforming pedagogic identities. Bernstein (2001) prompts us to look beyond the surface features of this pedagogic governance to consider the groups who are expected to acquire these pedagogic identities and the conditions in which these identities are to be acquired. We return to the notion of agents and agencies of symbolic control that were introduced earlier in this chapter to consider how PISA's "regime of global governance" (Meyer & Benavot, 2013, p. 7) influences local ITE programmes. From the OECD's perspective, ITE plays an important role in enacting PISA's policies (Lingard & Lewis, 2017) and shaping and reproducing these new pedagogic identities. For example, the OECD argues that there is a critical need for ITE to "address and support teachers' global competence development" (OECD, 2016, p. 19). It states that "teacher education and professional training are crucial to the successful implementation of global competence education" (p. 19) and, because of this, an entire section of the *Global competency for an inclusive world* framework (OECD, 2016) is dedicated to the development of Global Competence in teachers and teacher preparation programmes. It signals that the 2018 PISA will evaluate how well teacher education programmes prepare teachers to become "globally competent" (OECD, 2016, p. 3). As Bernstein (2000) points out, new pedagogical practices and curriculum content are easily acquired when there are systematic means through which to regulate acquisition. The OECD's intent to evaluate teacher education programmes signals a strong desire to ensure that ITE providers produce globally competent teachers who, in turn, can reproduce the OECD's interpretation of a globally competent student.

However, institutions such as ITE providers can also play an important role as shapers of ideas and knowledge and can be "a force for change and development" (Bernstein, 2001, p. 27). For this reason, agents operating within these institutions, such as teacher educators and academics, have the potential to disrupt the market-oriented socialisation of new pedagogic identities and restore notions of global competencies to their original intent. In other words, agencies such as ITE and actors such as pre-service teachers can be agents of change and transformation. It is here where Bernstein's conceptual tools allow us to understand the power of human agency to transform reproductive power structures, a notion that is central to critical realist ontology. But in what ways can teacher educators and ITE providers resist, disrupt and transform this market-driven orientation of global competences? How can ITE providers best prepare pre-service teachers to gain critical awareness of their work within an increasingly globalised society? To respond to these questions, we turn to the field of Comparative and International Education (CIE) to demonstrate how such scholarship can bring critical awareness to global processes, policies and reforms.

Making a Case for Comparative and International Education

Teacher education plays an important role in preparing pre-service teachers to have critical awareness of education reform. Zhao (2010) maintains that teachers "need to have a broad understanding of globalisation" so that they can "interpret the realities of globalisation on behalf of their students" (p. 426). He suggests that teachers should have critical awareness of the impact of international and government policies as well as the ability and courage to speak up to defend the future of their students. Teacher education can raise pre-service teachers' critical awareness by helping them understand "how broader social forces influence schooling and the curriculum" (Wang, Lin, Spalding, Odell, & Klecka, 2011, p. 116). This understanding can provide pre-service teachers with the capacity to identify, and the ability to resist and transform, changes to education policy, structures and curricula (Wang et al., 2011; Zhao, 2010).

The field of CIE provides a valuable foundation to prepare pre-service teachers to engage with these concerns. As CIE is "dedicated to increasing the understanding of educational issues, trends and policies, through comparative, cross-cultural and international perspectives" (Comparative and International Education, 2017, n. p.), it is well equipped to prepare pre-service teachers with this global awareness and critical insight in two important ways. Firstly, CIE can prepare pre-service teachers to gain greater critical awareness of their work within an increasingly globalised society (Robertson & Dale, 2015). When examining CIE programmes at the University of Auckland and Sydney University, Shah, McCormick and Thomas (2017) found that both programmes promoted an understanding of "the dialectic that exists between the local and global, but with clear attention to the tensions and clashes which neoliberal globalisation brings about…[and] critical deconstructions of binaries and taken for granted justificatory narratives" (p. 58). The intent to develop such a critical awareness of global and local influences on education is an important first step in resisting the production and reproduction of market-oriented pedagogic identities. In this regard, CIE can prepare pre-service teachers with the knowledge, skills, attitudes and behaviours to expose, critique and resist harmful educational reforms (Robertson, 2008, 2016).

Secondly, CIE can provide pre-service teachers with an authentic understanding of cross-cultural awareness. Much CIE scholarship places value on the cultural knowledge, values, practices and beliefs, and this has the potential for pre-service teachers to develop an authentic, rather than a market-driven interpretation of cross-cultural awareness. For example, O'Sullivan, Maarman, and Wolhuter (2010) found that pre-service teachers undertaking CIE classes in Ireland and South Africa developed a much broader and critical understanding of education, which strengthened teachers' abilities to teach in multicultural classrooms. This example is one of many which shows that CIE is an important field of scholarship for raising authentic, cross-cultural awareness of the dynamic relationships between global and local sites of education. It, therefore, has a powerful role to play in supporting agents such as academics, teacher educators and pre-service teachers with the knowledge to resist, disrupt and transform market-orientated interpretations of what it means to be a globally competent citizen.

Conclusion

Bernstein (2000) prompts us to make notions of power and control visible in any new educational reform so we can challenge and transform hidden assumptions that lead to unequal outcomes. In this chapter, we have identified and critiqued the socialising function of PISA's Global Competence and considered this in the light of the intended widespread reforms for ITE. Through a Bernsteinian analysis of the conceptual grammar within the OECD's *Global competency for an inclusive world* (OECD, 2016) framework, we have uncovered three key findings. Firstly, we conceptualised PISA's Global Competence as a pedagogic device to demonstrate how it has the capacity to act as a symbolic regulator of consciousness. We showed how this has the potential to rescript pedagogic identities to facilitate the production of human capital for the global labour market. Secondly, we demonstrated how PISA's Global Competence is one of several symbolic tools produced by the OECD to construct a new form of global pedagogic governance. We theorised that this shift reflects a move towards what Bernstein referred to as a TPS by aligning pedagogic governance with social control. Finally, we considered how ITE could play an important role in either reproducing or disrupting and transforming the socialising function of PISA's Global Competence. We suggest that the field of CIE is integral to support ITE programmes to (1) prepare pre-service teachers to gain greater critical awareness of their work within an increasingly globalised society; (2) prepare pre-service teachers with the knowledge, skills, attitudes and behaviours to expose, critique and resist harmful education reforms. In this way, we argue that engagement with CIE will better prepare pre-service teachers for uncertain futures within an increasingly globalised educational landscape.

References

Bernstein, B. (2000). *Pedagogy, symbolic control and identity: Theory, research, critique* (Revised Ed). Lanham: Rowman & Littlefield Publishers Inc.

Bernstein, B. (2001). Symbolic control: Issues of empirical description of agencies and agents. *International Journal of Social Research Methodology, 4*(1), 21–33.

Comparative and International Education. (2017). Comparative and International Education Society. http://www.cies.us.

Henry, M., Lingard, B., Rizvi, F., & Taylor, S. (2001). *The OECD, globalisation and education policy*. Oxford: IAU Press.

Labaree, D. F. (2014). Let's measure what no one teaches: PISA, NCLB, and the shrinking aims of education. *Teachers College Record, 116,* 1–14.

Lingard, B., & Lewis, S. (2017). Placing PISA and PISA for schools in two federalisms, Australia and the USA. *Critical Studies in Education, 58*(3), 1–14. https://doi.org/10.1080/17508487.2017.1316295.

Lingard, B., & Sellar, S. (2016). The changing organizational and global significance of the OECD's education work. *The Handbook of Global Education Policy,* 357–373. https://doi.org/10.1002/9781118468005.ch19.

Meyer, H.-D., & Benavot, A. (2013). PISA and the globalization of education governance: Some puzzles and problems. In H.-D. Meyer & A. Benavot (Eds.), *PISA, power, and policy: The emergence of global educational governance* (pp. 7–26). Oxford: Symposium Books Ltd.

Münch, R. (2014). Education under the regime of PISA & Co: Global standards and local traditions in conflict-The case of Germany. *Teachers College Record, 116,* 1–1.

Murphy, D. (2014). Issues with PISA's use of its data in the context of international education policy convergence. *Policy Futures in Education, 12*(7), 893–916. https://doi.org/10.2304/pfie.2014.12.7.893.

OECD. (2016). *Global competency for an inclusive world*. Paris: OECD.

OECD. (2017). *PISA 2015 assessment and analytical framework* (PISA). Paris: OECD: OECD Publishing. https://doi.org/10.1787/9789264281820-en.

O'Sullivan, M., Maarman, R. F., & Wolhuter, C. C. (2010). Primary student teachers' perceptions of and motivations for comparative education: Findings from a comparative study of an Irish and South African comparative education course. *Compare, 38,* 401–414.

Pykett, J. (2009). Pedagogical power: Lessons from school spaces. *Education, Citizenship and Social Justice, 4*(2), 102–116.

Robertson, S. L. (2008). "Remaking the World" neoliberalism and the transformation of education and teachers' Labor. In L. Weiner & M. Compton (Eds.), *The global assault on teaching, teachers, and their unions stories for resistance* (pp. 11–27). Basingstoke: Palgrave Macmillan. https://doi.org/10.1057/9780230611702.

Robertson, S. L. (2016). The global governance of teachers' work. In K. Mundy, A. Green, B. Lingard, & A. Verger (Eds.), *The handbook of global education policy* (pp. 275–290). West Sussex: John Wiley & Sons. https://doi.org/10.1002/9781118468005.ch15.

Robertson, S. L., & Dale, R. (2015). Towards a "critical cultural political economy" account of the globalising of education. *Globalisation, societies and education, 13*(1), 149–170. https://doi.org/10.1080/14767724.2014.967502.

Robertson, S. L., & Sorensen, T. (2017). Global transformations of the state, governance and teachers' labour: Putting Bernstein's conceptual grammar to work. *European Educational Research Journal, 0*(0), 1–19. https://doi.org/10.1177/1474904117724573.

Sellar, S., & Lingard, B. (2013). PISA and the expanding role of the OECD in global educational governance. In H.-D. Meyer (Ed.), *PISA, power, and policy: The emergence of global governance* (pp. 185–206). Oxford, United Kingdom: Symposium Books.

Sellar, S., & Lingard, B. (2014). The OECD and the expansion of PISA: New global modes of governance in education. *British Educational Research Journal, 40*(6), 917–936. https://doi.org/10.1002/berj.3120.

Shah, R., McCormick, A., & Thomas, M. A. M. (2017). Shifting tides: Reflecting on regional aspects of our roles as comparative and international educators. *The International Education Journal: Comparative Perspectives, 16*(3), 49–68.

Singh, P. (2015). Performativity and pedagogising knowledge: Globalising education policy formation, dissemination and enactment. *Journal of Education Policy, 30*(3), 363–384.

Singh, P. (2017). Pedagogic governance: Theorising with/after Bernstein. *British Journal of Sociology of Education, 38*(2), 144–163.

Tröhler, D., Meyer, H.-D., Labaree, D. F., & Hutt, E. (2014). Accountability: Antecedents, power, and processes. *Teachers College Record, 116,* 1–12.

Tyler, W. (2010). Towering TIMSS or leaning PISA? Vertical and horizontal models of international testing regimes. In P. Singh, A. R. Sadovnik, & S. F. Semel (Eds.), *Toolkits, translation devices and conceptual accounts: Essays on Basil Bernstein's sociology of knowledge* (pp 143 – 159). New York: Peter Lang.

Volante, L., & Fazio, X. (2018). PISA, policy, and global educational governance. In L. Volante (Ed.), *The PISA effect on global educational governance* (pp. 3–14). New York: Routledge.

Wang, J., Lin, E., Spalding, E., Odell, S. J., & Klecka, C. (2011). Understanding teacher education in an era of globalization. *Journal of Teacher Education, 62,* 115–120.

Woodward, R. (2009). *The Organisation for economic co-operation and development*. New York: Routledge.

Wiseman, A. W. (2013). Policy responses to PISA in comparative perspective. In H.-D. Meyer & A. Benavot (Eds.), *PISA, power, and policy: The emergence of global educational governance* (pp. 303–322). Oxford, U.K: Symposium Books.

Zhao, Y. (2010). Preparing globally competent teachers: A new imperative for teacher education. *Journal of Teacher Education, 61,* 422–431.

Author Biographies

Donella J. Cobb is a Lecturer in Te Hononga School of Curriculum and Pedagogy at The University of Waikato in Hamilton, New Zealand. Before coming to the University of Waikato, she was a teacher, Director of Music and Assistant Principal in primary schools in New Zealand, England and Australia. Her research centres around pedagogy and the contested notion of quality teaching. In the global context, she explores the cultural, political economy of education and the intersection between critical pedagogy and international education policy. Her current research examines the role of supranational organisations in the globalisation of learner-centred pedagogy. Within the New Zealand context, she has worked in collaboration with the Wilf Malcom Institute of Educational Research (WMIER) to study the development of teacher identity in pre-service teachers. She is particularly interested in the relationship between teacher identity, agency and the practicum context.

Daniel Couch is currently completing his Ph.D. at the University of Auckland. As an experienced Primary teacher and former Deputy Principal, his research interests include progressive theories of education and a global rise of neoliberal pedagogy. Much of his current research examines the relationship between systems of education within conflict affected contexts and the nation state. He is particularly interested in the influence of supranational actors and interests in driving education agendas within national education systems.

Chapter 4
Classroom-Ready Teachers: Who Is Responsible? Exploring Supervising Teacher Identity and Practice

Amanda Isaac and Suzanne Hudson

Abstract Initial teacher education (ITE) in Australia is currently under reform, particularly in light of the 2014 review by the Teacher Education Ministerial Advisory Group (TEMAG). This review renewed the call for the responsibility for ITE to be shared between schools and higher education providers. Since the work of supervising and assessing pre-service teachers (PST) in schools primarily falls to classroom teachers, this research explores the attitudes of a small group of supervising teachers towards shouldering this responsibility. It does this by adopting the lens of symbolic interactionism to examine the development of teacher educator identities among supervising teachers, the impact of environment and the supervising teachers' practices as a result of their identities. The data from the four one-to-one interviews highlight the teacher identities and how the teachers view themselves and their roles and responsibilities in ITE. The school environment is identified as an important enabling or disabling factor in effective supervision of PST. The results also draw attention to the relatively new issue of the assessment of PST against the Australian Professional Standards for Teachers (AITSL) and the supervising teachers' knowledge of and confidence with these Standards.

Keywords Initial teacher education · Teacher identities · Professional experience · Australian Professional Standards for Teachers · Supervising teachers

A. Isaac (✉)
Southern Cross University, Lismore, NSW, Australia
e-mail: Amanda.isaac@scu.edu.au

S. Hudson
Southern Cross University, Gold Coast, QLD, Australia
e-mail: Sue.hudson@scu.edu.au

© Springer Nature Singapore Pte Ltd. 2018   49
D. Heck and A. Ambrosetti (eds.), *Teacher Education In and For Uncertain Times*,
https://doi.org/10.1007/978-981-10-8648-9_4

Introduction

In a time of great change for education, the quality of initial teacher education (ITE) is under scrutiny in Australia and around the world. Over the last ten years, many reviews have been commissioned with the purpose of evaluating and analysing the effectiveness of the systems which prepare new teachers (Caldwell & Sutton, 2010; Carter, 2015; Donaldson, 2011). Their findings are often reflected in policies which present new challenges for those involved in ITE.

One of the emerging principles of the 2014 Australian report into initial teacher education entitled *Classroom Ready Teachers* (Teacher Education Ministerial Advisory Group [TEMAG], 2014) is that "Initial teacher education providers, teacher employers and schools must share a commitment to improve initial teacher education and work in partnership to achieve strong graduate and student outcomes" (TEMAG, 2014, p. ix). This statement implies a willingness from all contributors to work towards this improvement. Another focus outlined is the need for "robust evidence that all graduate teachers meet the Graduate level of the Professional Standards" (TEMAG, 2014, p. x). Amidst such calls for shared commitment to ITE, and measurable evidence of pre-service teachers' (PST) "classroom readiness", is uncertainty around where the responsibility lies for both the teaching and the assessment of PST during professional experience or practicum.

In an attempt to address this uncertainty, this chapter focuses on the important role of the supervising teachers who work with the PSTs during their professional experience placements. It will discuss a small-scale research project, with the research aim:—*To what extent do supervising teachers see themselves as responsible for ITE?* The research questions are:

1. How do supervising teachers define their role in ITE?
2. What tasks do supervising teachers perceive as their responsibility in ITE?
3. What tasks do supervising teachers perceive as the university's responsibility in ITE?
4. What are some factors that support or hinder supervising teachers' commitment to ITE?

In the research, supervising teachers are asked about what they see as their responsibility to teach PST during professional experience and how they feel about assessing PST against the Australian Professional Standards for Teachers (Australian Institute of Teaching and School Leadership [AITSL], 2014a). The discussion leads to the identification of a variety of developing initial teacher educator identities within the role of supervising teacher.

Literature Review

Reflecting international trends, over the last fifteen years in Australia, public interest in the quality of ITE has remained high. Elliott-Johns suggests that decisions around how universities and education systems prepare teachers have become "everyone's business" (2015, p. 99). As a result, state and federal governments, as well as other key stakeholders, have commissioned multiple reviews of ITE. A common element in the findings from all these reviews is the importance of sound relationships between schools and higher education providers (House of Representatives Standing Committee on Education and Vocational Training [HRSCEVT], 2007; Caldwell & Sutton, 2010; TEMAG, 2014).

Despite all the positive rhetoric, there is ample evidence that the forming of partnerships in ITE is far from simple. TEMAG admonishes universities and schools for "not effectively working together in the development of new teachers" (2014, p. ix), whilst Caldwell and Sutton (2010, p. xix) recognise that there are "sound intentions" on the part of key stakeholders; they highlight that this does not guarantee a positive experience for PST. More recently, Le Cornu confirmed the need for high-quality partnerships, describing them as "those that involve a shared responsibility by the stakeholders for ITE and a willingness to work together" (2015, p. 16). She added that the changes required for both "restructuring" and "reculturing", as a result of recommendations from TEMAG (2014) will take considerable time and effort (Le Cornu, 2015, p. 17). Considering that any changes to professional experience will significantly impact on the work of supervising teachers, it would be helpful to listen to their experiences and insights into professional experience to inform future policy.

Perceptions of Supervision of ITE as a Professional Responsibility

There exists conflicting evidence on the question of whether supervising teachers, as major stakeholders in professional experience, see their involvement in ITE as a facet of their professional responsibility (Lynch & Smith, 2012). Iancu-Haddad & Oplatka (2009) suggest that teachers' views about their responsibility to mentor PST are more complex, with external forces placing extrinsic motivations which may then develop into intrinsic, more altruistic incentives as relationships develop and benefits emerge. Supervising teachers' views are impacted by a number of influences, some personal and some environmental.

For example, the attitudes a supervising teacher takes into the mentoring relationship have profound impacts (Ambrosetti & Dekkers, 2010). Research shows these attitudes are quite individual, influenced by past experiences of mentoring, including personality matches (or mismatches) with PST, and past successes or failures (Kwan & Lopez-Real, 2005; Uusimaki, 2013). Van Velzen, Volman, Brekelmans, and White (2012) refer to a number of reasons why teachers may be reticent to accept a supervisory role, including the idea that they may feel that their practical knowledge is undervalued in comparison to 'university knowledge' and an underlying attitude of individualism, where "going into a teacher's classroom is considered an intrusion" (p. 231). One of the deciding factors of whether a teacher sees it as his/her responsibility to supervise a PST may be whether or not this task aligns with his/her sense of what it means to be a professional. However, it is difficult to find current literature that has asked if this is so.

The willingness of teachers to take on supervisory roles can also be linked to how the role is perceived by others (Levine, 2011). If it is valued and rewarded, teachers are more willing to take on the extra work that it entails. Factors such as recognition of teachers' supervisory work with PST from executive staff (Ievers et al., 2013), training for the role (Bradbury & Koballa, 2008; Hudson & Bird, 2015) and financial reimbursement are examples of how this has been achieved. Clarke, Triggs and Nielson also point out that "Co-operating teachers are first and foremost teachers of children" (2014, p. 185). They are balancing their ITE role with this primary responsibility (Graham, 2006). In an already busy job, many teachers believe that it is unrealistic to take on the responsibility for teaching yet another learner.

Assessing Pre-service Teachers' "Classroom Readiness" Using the Australian Professional Standards for Teachers

A recurring theme in research on how supervising teachers see themselves as stake-holders within ITE is the confusion around the role of the supervising teacher. This is well documented in the literature, manifesting itself in ample discourse around teachers' roles as 'mentors' versus 'supervisors' (e.g. Ambrosetti & Dekkers, 2010; Hudson & Millwater, 2008). The debates around these two terms seek to clarify the responsibilities of the supervising teacher in the seemingly conflicting task of set-ting up a supportive relationship with the PST in order to support and guide them, whilst simultaneously serving the role of assessor of their PST 'classroom readiness'. Some papers set up these roles as a dichotomy, suggesting that one has preference over the other (Christie, Conlon, Gemmell, & Long, 2004). However, more fre-quently in current research (Ievers et al., 2013; Levine, 2011; Spendlove, Howes, & Wake, 2010), the words of Ambrosetti and Dekkers (2010, p. 43) are reflected; "Despite the highlighted differences between mentoring and supervision, mentors in pre-service teacher education engage in both mentoring and supervisory roles". Supervising teachers are commonly seen as the most pivotal influence on a PST success in professional experience (McCarthy & Quinn, 2010), and yet they often express a lack of confidence in what it is that they are expected to do. It could be argued that confidence in assessing PST competence will be addressed as supervis-ing teachers become increasingly familiar with the Australian Professional Standards for Teachers (AITSL, 2014a). Universities and school systems now have a common set of criteria and a shared language around teacher competency against which PST are measured. Indeed, Recommendation 23 of the TEMAG report states that "Sys-tems/schools be required to use the Australian Professional Standards for Teachers in identifying highly skilled teachers to supervise professional experience" (2014, p. 33), whilst Recommendation 25 dictates that "Higher education providers assess all pre-service teachers against the Graduate level of the Professional Standards" (p. 39). However, in this uncertain period of determination what may or may not constitute as evidence against the Australian Professional Standards for Teachers (AITSL, 2011), the appropriateness of their use as a "control device" (Buchanan, 2017, p. 123) may be questioned. Spendlove, Howes and Wake warn, from a UK perspective, that the difference between the interpretation of professional Standards by supervising teachers and university-based educators can lead to breakdowns in partnerships and "an impoverished view of what it is to be a professional" (2010, p. 75). Indeed, some research indicates that the discourse around the use of the Australian Professional Standards for Teachers (AITSL, 2011; AITSL, 2014a) for assessing PST "emphasises a divide between the university and school components of initial teacher education" (Leonard, 2012, p. 60) which is the very opposite to what was intended. As part of the research presented in this chapter, the experiences and views of a number of supervising teachers regarding their use of Australian Professional Standards for Teachers (AITSL, 2011) as assessment criteria for "teacher-readiness" will be presented.

Teachers' Identity as 'School-Based Initial Teacher Educators'

The development of teacher identity is a well-researched area, particularly in regard to newly graduated teachers as they move into the classroom as professionals (Beauchamp & Thomas, 2011; Morrison, 2014; Roehriga, Bohnb, Turnerc, & Pressley, 2008). However, research into more experienced classroom teachers' sense of identity as educators of PST focuses more on teachers within the higher education system, particularly those moving from the school sector (Klopper & Power, 2014; McDonough & Brandenburg, 2012; Murray, 2014; White, 2014). Whilst some would say that, within discussions of ITE teacher identity, "the voices of mentor/cooperating teachers are noticeably absent" (Clift, 2017, p. 225), some work has been done to remedy this imbalance. Forgasz (2017) focuses on supervising teacher's experiences through self-study research, alluding to the change in university-based educator identities implicit in the development of the new idea of supervising teachers as "school-based teacher educators" (p. 219). The research presented in this chapter seeks to contribute to the exploration of these growing teacher identities.

Conceptual Framework

In this chapter, a conceptual model based on symbolic interactionism (Dillon, 2013) structures the discussion of the findings and makes meaningful links between the research questions. Blumer, the father of symbolic interactionism said, "Human beings act toward things on the basis of the meanings that the things have for them" (as cited in Flick, 2009, p. 58). The research sought to explore how participants' view their identity as initial teacher educators and how this impacts on what they see as their responsibility to do as supervising teachers. Tracy (2013) explains the codependence that symbolic interactionism gives to identity, action and environment. Does a teacher's involvement in ITE (action) mean they see themselves as responsible as initial teacher educators (identity)? What factors (environment) contribute to the perception of this identity as an initial teacher educator?

Methods

Sampling Decisions

Purposive sampling (Punch, 2009) was utilised for this project with the deliberate choice of four primary school teachers who had previously demonstrated a commitment to ITE by mentoring at least five PSTs. These particular participants were selected because of their ability to "purposefully inform an understanding of the research problem" (Creswell, 2013, p. 156). The fact that these teachers were local and known to the researcher through their involvement in a regional university professional experience program, also ensured the ready access and ease of contact typical of convenience sampling (Punch, 2009). The sample included a mix of male and female respondents, across Catholic and public schools systems, with a variety of teaching experience (10–21 years).

Data Collection and Analysis

The project utilised semi-structured one-to-one interviewing as a method of data collection. Interviews were arranged at times and venues convenient to the participants. Giving participants the control over these two factors was designed to go some way to addressing any negative consequences of "the interviewer effect" (Denscombe, 2010, p. 278) which may have been felt by participants who had worked with the researcher in professional experience programs.

Interviews, ranging from 25 min to one hour, were recorded using a video recorder which assisted in the accuracy of transcription. The data were then analysed using the logical sequence of steps appropriate for qualitative data outlined by Creswell (2013). The names of the teachers and their associated schools were de-identified to maintain privacy as an ethical consideration and to allow the teachers to speak freely (Creswell, 2013). Data were organised initially under research question headings to ensure "coherence of the material" and focus on central issues within the research (Cohen, Manion, & Morrison, 2007, p. 468). The small number of participants negated any need for software, so all data analysis was manual.

Throughout the transcription of the interviews and on a first reading of the data, memos were recorded, noting common ideas or contradictions. The data were then coded, and contrasts and comparisons were drawn. For some research questions, tables of participant responses were designed. The researcher moved between the data, the initial record of ideas and the identified themes a number of times to seek meaning in the participants' responses, as central ideas began to be clarified with further analysis.

In order to describe the data, a one-page summary identifying the themes for each research question was compiled. This included supporting quotes from the interviews. In an example of iterative analysis (Srivastava & Hopwood, 2009), these themes were then incorporated under the relevant research question, to ensure that the data were addressing the overarching research aim.

Addressing Validity and Reliability

As a part of the implementation of any research project, its worthiness and scholarly value must be evaluated with honesty and rigour. The qualitative nature of this project required this to be approached through the examination of the credibility, transferability and confirmability of the research process.

To ensure its authenticity through an examination of credibility, member checks were incorporated into the research process three to four weeks after the interviews. Participants were offered the opportunity to read the findings chapter to check the accuracy of the researcher's interpretation of what they had expressed, before the discussion chapter was written. No changes were requested by any participant. This not only gave value to what participants had shared but was an important process to guarantee that their perceptions and experiences had been accurately captured by the research.

As far as its applicability to other contexts, the researcher adopted the stance of Lincoln and Guber (as cited in Cohen et al., 2007) that the responsibility of a qualitative researcher does not lay in guaranteeing external validity, but in providing quality data and analysis to enable readers to make their own decisions about its generalisability. This sample does not attempt to be representative, but the research, in presenting thick descriptive data, should enable "the reader to judge the transferability of findings to other situations" (Punch, 2009, p. 316). Confirmability has been maximised through carefully written letters and discussions with participants outlining research purposes, audience and possible outcomes.

Findings

Teacher Identities in ITE

In seeking to address Research Question 1: *How do supervising teachers define their role?*, participants were asked to define their role in ITE and present ways in which they support PST during professional experience. Responses confirmed and expanded current literature with the roles of supportive mentor and model of teaching practice being expressed by all supervising teachers (Ambrosetti & Dekkers, 2010; Clarke, Triggs, & Neilson, 2014; Hudson & Bird, 2015). The three more experienced participants also highlighted the importance of allowing their PST to develop their own teacher identity. Participant 3 expressed this as being able to let go of control "…so that they can put their own spin, begin to find their own teaching style in the classroom and develop their own way of adapting to the profession." The participants presented varied responses in regards to their views about assessing PST. Through their responses, participants gave insights into not only how they saw themselves in the role of supervising teacher, but also from where these perceptions of identity originated. Symbolic interactionism is useful when analysing roles (Turner, Abercrombie, & Hill, 2006) and, in this research particularly, looking at the factors behind the evolution of these roles.

The development of participants' identities as 'initial teacher educators' was clearly impacted by their experiences of engaging in professional experience as PST themselves. All four participants identified either positive or negative experiences (Johnston, 2010) as instrumental in them volunteering to supervise PST. This, in turn, influenced how they perceived their role. For example Participant 4 who related stories of her own professional experience in which she felt "useless" and "confused", saw her role in terms of providing both professional and personal support. "You're really caring for them" and "It's a bit like being a Mum." Participant 3 who recalled working very hard to achieve excellent results as a PST expressed her role in terms of setting high expectations. "I normally tell them what I expect…I tell them that if I don't have a lesson plan on my desk in the morning then I'm not going to be impressed."

In addition, participants' experiences of supervising a number of PST affected the way in which they expressed their sense of identity in this role. This is particularly the case when participants related stories of supervising PST who had struggled to satisfy requirements for professional experience. Supervising teachers' reactions to this challenge varied, with some participants feeling their primary role in this situation as "gatekeeper to the profession" (Clarke et al., 2014) or "quality controller" (Kwan & Lopez-Real, 2005). Others saw this as an opportunity to mentor PST to success (Graham, 2006; Hall, Draper, Smith, & Bullough, 2008). Symbolic interactionism describes this development of identity through interaction with others as a complex and dynamic process. "I know who I am and I know how to respond and behave in a given situation because I have learned from others' attitudes toward me" (Dillon, 2013, p. 275). There were quite different perceptions of the role of supervising teacher, and they were found to have a significant impact on how the participants then carried out their role in ITE.

The responses to this research question closely reflected the current research on roles of supervising teachers (Ambrosetti & Dekkers, 2010; Hall et al., 2008; Hudson & Millwater, 2008). This included the conflicts teachers had about their professional identities within ITE when they recognised their responsibility to both mentor and assess PST classroom readiness. Participant 4 said, "I have a problem in that I'm too positive. I find it difficult unless I talk to someone like you (researcher) who is their supervisor who can ask those really defined questions". However, it is difficult to find research like this, which has sought to understand the reasons behind the differences in teachers' interpretations of the role of supervising teacher and what impact this may have on their supervising practice or priorities.

How Teacher Identities Impact Teacher Action in ITE

Another way in which this project examined teachers' sense of their responsibility in ITE was through Research Questions 2 and 3—What tasks do supervising teachers perceive as their responsibility in ITE? What tasks do supervising teachers perceive as the university's responsibility in ITE?

Symbolic interactionism sees significance in the interaction between how people see themselves, or their identity, as discussed above, and the resulting ways in which they act. This is described as "agency and action" by Denzin (2004, p. 120). This interaction was clearly demonstrated when participants were asked to name the skills, knowledge and attitudes which were their responsibility to teach to PST and which were the responsibility of the university. These research questions yielded a great variance in responses which mirrored some of the literature around the lack of communication between schools and universities about expectations of supervising teachers (Bradbury & Koballa, 2008; Christie et al., 2004; Jaipal, 2009). However, what was interesting was how the participants' individual answers aligned closely with their expressions of initial teacher educator identities.

Participants concurred that some aspects of the profession, like behaviour management and working with the curriculum, were their responsibility to teach PST. However, it was the differences in responses, which illustrated that agency results in particular actions. For example, Participant 1, who saw the supervising teacher role in terms of explicit modelling and provision of feedback, emphasised the responsibility to pass on practical skills like setting up programs and choosing appropriate resources. In contrast, Participant 4, who described her identity as a supervising teacher in more personal and supportive terms, named the development of relational skills such as diplomacy and professionalism, along with the encouragement of a positive attitude, as important things to teach. Participant 3, who identified as a supervising teacher who mentors PSTs into working within the school community said this, "It's my responsibility to actually allow the PST to see what the whole teacher role is and it's my job to be able to take them with me, introduce them to community members, have conversations, see my discussions, be a part of community events that happen within the school." When asking the question of the extent to which teachers see themselves as responsible for ITE, it is interesting to see the differences between the perceptions of their responsibilities, and how these are influenced, not so much by a guide or checklist provided by the university, but by the priorities of the individuals, based on their sense of identity as an initial teacher educator.

Participants 3 and 4 mainly identified areas of knowledge that should be taught by universities: "understanding curriculum, understanding programming, societies in context (things like that)", reflecting their own sense of responsibility as being to pass on practical skills and attitudes during professional experience. In contrast, those who identified as models of pedagogy and providers of assessment expected skills and attitudes to be taught in the higher education setting. Participant 1 expected the university to "teach correct structure of planning and programming. I don't think that's our responsibility as teachers. I think they need to come into the school knowing that already", whilst Participant 2 stated "It's the university's responsibility to make clear the expectations of the prac with regard to things like preparation and being professional" Interviews suggested these views emerged from negative experiences with supervising PST. Johnston's work on difficult professional experience placements, advocates that the university has a role in "making students aware of the importance of developing strong working bonds with teachers and helping them develop a repertoire of strategies that will enable them to interact positively with colleagues" (2010, p. 318). The responsibility for teaching the complex combination of knowledge, skills and attitudes required to become a teacher is not something that can be clearly divided between the providers of ITE in higher education and school settings. Nevertheless, it is useful to look at the motivations that underpin whether teachers see themselves as responsible and how the perception of their identity influences their associated practice towards mentoring PST.

The Impact of Environment on the Development of ITE Identities

In the investigation of supervising teachers' sense of responsibility in ITE, Research Question 4 was posed:—*What are some factors that support or hinder supervising teachers' commitment to ITE?*

Responses contributed to an overall picture of teacher experiences and possible directions for encouraging others to take on the responsibility of teacher identities in ITE. Symbolic interactionism acknowledges the impact that environment has on how people develop their identities and how they enact these identities. "We interact with ourselves and others differently in different social environments because of the different meanings and expectations characterizing those contexts" (Dillon, 2013, p. 218). This research raised three main points when looking at what factors supported or hindered participants in terms of the social environments of ITE.

School Community in Which the Participant Operated

Different participants raised the level of support given by the whole school community to themselves as supervising teacher and to their PST, as a factor of support or hindrance to their role. Participant 3 explained, "It's not just me who takes the student on, *we* take a student on. Yeah, they follow me around but the support the staff gives a PST is important." Conversely, Participant 4 said, "It's hard when there are multiple colleagues to interact with and they are not prepared to guide your allocated prac student in tandem with you, or in the rare case of your absence." If initial teacher educator identities are developed through interactions, there seems an argument for greater collaboration around ITE within school communities. These findings support a number of pieces of research which advocate the idea of groups of supervising teachers developing a 'community of practice' or the development of approaches which see PST supervised by a team of teachers, rather than one (Johnston, 2010). This is an area in which further research and trialling of alternative models of supervision would be useful.

Relationship with the University

Again, in both positive and negative terms, participants identified their relationship with the university as a factor that either encouraged or discouraged them to take on the identity of an initial teacher educator in the school setting. All participants stated that well-prepared students and clear guidelines from the university as key influence on their sense of agency as supervising teachers. Whether satisfied or dissatisfied with their experiences with the university, participants agreed that early communication from university staff to clarify expectations, along with support with the task of assessing PST against the Australian Professional Standards for Teachers (AITSL, 2011), would help supervising teachers to feel more confident in taking on the responsibility of ITE.

The interviewees' sense of satisfaction with PST preparedness reflected the teacher identities highlighted above. Those who prioritised relationship building and development of the PST professional self seemed happy with the university preparation, working from the point of their PST readiness. In contrast, the "gatekeeper" participants expressed dissatisfaction at having to take responsibility for what they perceived as the role of the university. Research which draws attention to misunderstanding of the role and responsibilities of universities and schools in ITE is not new (Bradbury & Koballa, 2008; Christie et al., 2004; Lynch & Smith, 2012). However, this research has raised the idea of the intrinsic link between how teachers see their identity as a supervisor of PST and the extent to which they see themselves responsible for certain tasks within this role. If schools and universities worked together to explore, articulate and value this unique identity of initial teacher educator in the school setting, teachers might be more open to taking on this responsibility as a partner in ITE.

The Implementation of the APST

The implementation of the Australian Professional Standards for Teachers (AITSL, 2014a) as the assessment criteria for the professional experience component of ITE (AITSL, 2011; TEMAG, 2014) was seen as an enabler or a hindrance by different participants in this research. Those who had graduated since the introduction of the Australian Professional Standards for Teachers (AITSL, 2014a) felt comfortable with using them as both a formative and summative assessment tool. Conversely, the two participants who had graduated at an earlier date, and who have not yet reaccredited, were less confident (AITSL, 2014b). Participant 3 saw it as a challenge and opportunity to become familiar with the Standards for ongoing professional development, "The (Standard) descriptors are good…they help me know what I've got be teaching". However, Participant 4 saw the reporting of PST against the Australian Professional Standards for Teachers (AITSL, 2011) as a hindrance to her fulfilling her perceived role, "I'm happy to judge if someone has what it takes but I wish I didn't have to use the Standards. I want to be able to really say what they can do and where they sit and ticking boxes about teaching Standards tells you nothing". Both nationally and internationally, recent literature notes this same tension (Bahr & Mellor, 2016; Hudson, 2009; Spendlove et al., 2010). Supervising teachers' attitudes towards assessing against the Australian Professional Standards for Teachers (AITSL, 2014a) is an area which could be explored in greater depth as this variance in supervising teachers' views about using these Standards has an impact on the extent to which they feel responsible in ITE. If teachers embrace the Australian Professional Standards for Teachers as a valid framework for evaluating professional competency (AITSL, 2011), they may be more willing to share this task of evaluating PST with higher education providers. However, if teachers have not invested in the value of the Australian Professional Standards for Teachers as an evaluative tool, or feel that their professional judgement is being undervalued, they will be less likely to accept responsibility within an ITE program.

Conclusions and Implications

This research proposes that the extent to which teachers feel responsible for ITE is determined by their own initial teacher identity, which has been formed by a complex combination of personal experiences and environmental factors. Since environmental factors are the only variables that to some extent may be controlled, this research has significance for the development of more effective models of professional experience within ITE, based on changes to these environmental factors.

Recognition of the Valuable Role of Supervising Teachers in ITE

The first implication from this study regards the role of universities and school systems in the recognition of supervising teachers as vital school-based initial teacher educators. As new initial teacher educator identities are developed, it will be essential to promote and value these. One way is a recognition of the importance of training supervising teachers for their important role in ITE (Hudson, 2010; McQuillin, Straight, & Saeki, 2015). Training programs already exist for supervising teachers (e.g. Mentoring for Effective Teaching; AITSL Supervising Teacher Modules). However, such programs need to be continually updated to address the changing nature of ITE and be made readily available to supervising teachers with incentives for completion. Another area for consideration is further recognition of this role within the model of professional accreditation. Supervising teachers are rewarded financially, but there is room to explore systems for rewarding them professionally, both informally and formally (Price & Willett, 2006; Uusimaki, 2013; Walkington, 2007). Perhaps promotional positions could be made available or specific positions introduced in effective mentoring. If teachers are to be expected to share in the responsibility of initial teacher education as highlighted in the literature, then government bodies need to explore new ways to recognise and reward teachers who are willing to share their experience and expertise.

A Collaborative Approach to the Supervision of PST

The findings of this research emphasise the impact of the school community on a teacher's experience of their school-based initial teacher educator identity. The implication is that if the school environment is more collaborative in its approach to ITE, teachers would be more confident to take on the responsibility of supervising a PST. It would be interesting to investigate PST perceptions of collaboration in school communities and its impact on their experience. Some work has been done on implementing pilot programs which incorporate collaborative supervisory roles (Johnston, 2010). However, further studies could be done on investigating the characteristics and practices of existing supportive school communities, to design professional experience placement systems in which both the PST and the supervising teacher are well supported. By developing a whole school community model for better supporting PST and supervising teacher during professional experience, other schools could adopt and adapt the model to enhance the practices within their own contexts.

Using the APST to Assess Classroom Readiness

The findings have highlighted a tension in the implementation of the Australian Professional Standards for Teachers (AITSL, 2014a) in the area of professional experience in ITE. Despite efforts to familiarise teachers with the Standards, the findings of this research suggest that not all supervising teachers are convinced of their usefulness as a tool for assessing PST on their classroom readiness. New ways need to be explored to support supervising teachers to have a deeper understanding of the Australian Professional Standards for Teachers and how they can be used to effectively assess PST development and demonstrate evidence of practice. Universities can play a vital role by providing professional learning for teachers which will further enhance the school–university partnerships advocated in the literature and ITE reviews. Whether they are comfortable using the Standards or not, the introduction of the Australian Professional Standards for Teachers has changed the way supervising teachers see and feel about their role, and therefore enact it. Whilst there is some research into teachers' attitudes towards evaluating their own practice against the Australian Professional Standards for Teachers (AITSL, 2014b), there is little literature around their experiences, views and approaches to assessing PST. By exploring supervising teachers' experiences of using the Standards as an assessment tool, further information can be gathered to better understand and evaluate the implementation of the Australian Professional Standards for Teachers in ITE.

To sum up, this research provides a worthwhile contribution to the discussion of developing supervising teacher identities within the changing landscape of ITE and professional standards. Limitations include the small scale of the study and the researcher's knowledge of participants. However, the findings indicate that further work on a larger scale could build on understandings of the changing identities of initial teacher educators within the school setting.

References

Ambrosetti, A., & Dekkers, J. (2010). The interconnectedness of the roles of mentors and mentees in pre-service teacher education mentoring relationships. *Australian Journal of Teacher Education, 35*(6), 42–55.

Australian Institute for Teaching and School Leadership [AITSL]. (2011). *Accreditation of initial teacher education programs in Australia: Standards and procedures.* https://www.aitsl.edu.au/deliver-ite-programs/standards-and-procedures.

Australian Institute for Teaching and School Leadership [AITSL]. (2014a). *Professional standards for teachers.* Retrieved from http://aitsl.edu.au/australian-professional-standards-for-teachers/standards/list.

Australian Institute for Teaching and School Leadership [AITSL]. (2014b). *Evaluation of the implementation of the Australian professional standards for teachers: Interim report on baseline implementation 2013 key findings.* https://www.aitsl.edu.au/docs/default-source/default-document-library/evaluation-of-the-implementation-of-the-australian-professional-standards-for-teachers—interim-report-on-baseline-implementation.pdf?sfvrsn=7a8aec3c_0.

Bahr, N., & Mellor, S. (2016). *Building quality in teaching and teacher education*. Camberwell, Australia: Australian Council for Educational Research.

Beauchamp, C., & Thomas, L. (2011). New teachers' identity shifts at the boundary of teacher education and initial practice. *International Journal of Educational Research, 50*(1), 6–13.

Bradbury, L., & Koballa, T. (2008). Borders to cross: Identifying sources of tension in mentor-intern relationships. *Teaching and Teacher Education: An International Journal of Research and Studies, 24*(8), 2132–2145. https://doi.org/10.1016/j.tate.2008.03.002.

Buchanan, J. (2017). How do the standards stand up? Applying quality teacher frameworks to the Australian Professional Standards. In J. Nuttall, A. Kostogriz, M. Jones, & J. Martin (Eds.), *Teacher education policy and practice: Evidence of impact, impact of evidence* (pp. 115–128). Singapore: Springer.

Caldwell, B., & Sutton, D. (2010). *Review of teacher education: First report-full report*. Retrieved from http://education.qld.gov.au/students/higher-education/resources/review-teacher-education-school-induction-first-full-report.pdf.

Carter, E. (2015). *Carter review of initial teacher training*. Retrieved from https://www.gov.uk/government/uploads/system/…/Carter_Review.pdf.

Christie, F., Conlon, T., Gemmell, T., & Long, A. (2004). Effective partnership? Perceptions of PGCE student teacher supervision. *European Journal of Teacher Education, 27*(2), 109–123. https://doi.org/10.1080/0261976042000222999.

Clarke, A., Triggs, V., & Nielson, W. (2014). Cooperating teacher participation in teacher education: A review of the literature. *Review of Educational Research, 84*(2), 163–202. https://doi.org/10.3102/0034654313499618.

Clift, R. T. (2017). Missing voices in the study of the practicum. *Studying Teacher Education, 13*(2), 225–230. https://doi.org/10.1080/17425964.2017.1342979.

Cohen, L., Manion, L., & Morrison, K. (2007). *Research methods in education* (6th ed.). Milton Park: Routledge.

Creswell, J. (2013). *Qualitative inquiry and research design: Choosing among five approaches* (3rd ed.). Thousand Oaks, CA: Sage.

Denscombe, M. (2010). *Good research guide for small-scale social research projects*. Berkshire: McGraw-Hill.

Denzin, N. (2004). Symbolic interactionism. In U. Flick, E. von Kardoff, & I. Steinke (Eds.), *A companion to qualitative research*. London: Sage.

Dillon, M. (2013). *Introduction to sociological theory: Theorists, concepts, and their applicability to the twenty-first century*. Milton, QLD: John Wiley & Sons.

Donaldson, G. (2011). *Teaching Scotland's future—Report of a review of teacher education in Scotland*. Retrieved from http://www.gov.scot/Publications/2011/01/13092132/0.

Elliott-Johns, S. (2015). Coda: Insights gleaned from the voices of deans in education. In S. Elliott-Johns (Ed.), *Leadership for change in teacher education: Voices of Canadian Deans of Education*. Sense: Rotterdam.

Flick, U. (2009). *An introduction to qualitative research* (4th ed.). London: Sage.

Forgasz, R. (2017). Seeing teacher education differently through self-study of professional practice. *Studying Teacher Education, 13*(2), 216–224. https://doi.org/10.1080/17425964.2017.1342360.

Graham, B. (2006). Conditions for successful field experiences: Perceptions of cooperating teachers. *Teaching and Teacher Education, 22*, 1118–1129.

Hall, K. M., Draper, R. J., Smith, L. K., & Bullough, R. V., Jr. (2008). More than a place to teach: Exploring the perceptions of the roles and responsibilities of mentor teachers. *Mentoring & Tutoring: Partnership in Learning, 16*(3), 328–345. https://doi.org/10.1080/1361126082231708.

House of Representatives Standing Committee on Education and Vocational Training [HRSCEVT]. (2007). *Top of the class: Report on the inquiry into teacher education*. (978-0-642-78894-8). Canberra: House of Representatives Publishing Unit.

Hudson, P. (2009). How can preservice teachers be measured against advocated professional teaching standards? *Australian Journal of Teacher Education, 34*(5), 65–73.

Hudson, P. (2010). Mentors report on their own mentoring practices. *Australian Journal of Teacher Education, 35*(7), 30–42.

Hudson, P., & Bird, L. (2015). Investigating a model of mentoring for effective teaching. *Journal of Teaching Effectiveness and Student Achievement, 2*(2), 11–21.

Hudson, P., & Millwater, J. (2008). Mentors' views about developing effective English teaching practices. *Australian Journal of Teacher Education, 33*(5), 1–13.

Iancu-Haddad, D., & Oplatka, I. (2009). Mentoring novice teachers: Motives, process and outcomes from the mentor's point of view. *The New Educator, 5*(1), 45–65.

Ievers, M., Wylie, K., Gray, C., Ní Áingléis, B., & Cummins, B. (2013). The role of the university tutor in school-based work in primary schools in Northern Ireland and the Republic of Ireland. *European Journal of Teacher Education, 36*(2), 183–199. https://doi.org/10.1080/02619768.2012.687718.

Jaipal, K. (2009). Re-envisioning mentorship: Pre-service teachers and associate teachers as co-learners. *Teaching Education, 20*(3), 257–276.

Johnston, D. (2010). 'Losing the joy': Student teachers' experiences of problematic relations with host teachers on school placement. *Teacher Development, 14*(3), 307–320. https://doi.org/10.1080/13664530.2010.504012.

Klopper, C. J., & Power, B. M. (2014). The casual approach to teacher education: what effect does casualisation have for Australian University Teaching? *Australian Journal of Teacher Education, 39*(4), 101–114.

Kwan, T., & Lopez-Real, F. (2005). Mentors' perceptions of their roles in mentoring student teachers. *Asia-Pacific Journal of Teacher Education, 33*(3), 275–287. https://doi.org/10.1080/13598660500286267.

Le Cornu, R. (2015). *Key components of effective professional experience in initial teacher education in Australia*. Melbourne: Australian Institute for Teaching and School Leadership.

Leonard, S. (2012). Professional conversations: Mentor teachers' theories-in-use using the Australian National Professional Standards for Teachers. *An International Journal of Teacher Education, 37*(12), 46–62.

Levine, T. (2011). Features and strategies of supervisor professional community as a means of improving the supervision of preservice teachers. *Teaching and Teacher Education, 27*(5), 930–941. https://doi.org/10.1016/j.tate.2011.03.004.

Lynch, D., & Smith, R. (2012). Teacher education partnerships: An Australian research-based perspective. *Australian Journal of Teacher Education, 37*(11). https://doi.org/10.14221/ajte.2012v37n11.7.

McCarthy, J., & Quinn, L. (2010). Supervision in teacher education. *International encyclopedia of education* (pp. 615–621). https://doi.org/10.1016/b978-0-08-044894-7.00667-9.

McDonough, S., & Brandenburg, R. (2012). Examining assumptions about teacher educator identities by self-study of the role of mentor of pre-service teachers. *Studying Teacher Education, 8*(2), 169–182. https://doi.org/10.1080/17425964.2012.692990.

McQuillin, S. D., Straight, G. G., & Saeki, E. (2015). Program support and value of training in mentors' satisfaction and anticipated continuation of school-based mentoring relationships. *Mentoring & Tutoring: Partnership in Learning, 23*(2), 133–148. https://doi.org/10.1080/13611267.2015.1047630.

Morrison, C. (2014). Teacher identity in the early career phase: Trajectories that explain and influence development. *Australian Journal of Teacher Education, 38*(4), 91–107. https://doi.org/10.14221/ajte.2013v38n4.5.

Murray, J. (2014). Teacher educators' constructions of professionalism: a case study. *Asia-Pacific Journal of Teacher Education, 42*(1), 7–21. https://doi.org/10.1080/1359866X.2013.870971.

Price, A., & Willett, J. (2006). Primary teachers' perceptions of the impact of initial teacher training upon primary schools. *Journal of In-Service Education, 32*(1), 33–45. https://doi.org/10.1080/13674580500480057.

Punch, K. (2009). *Introduction to research methods in education*. London: Sage.

Roehriga, A., Bohnb, C., Turnerc, J., & Pressley, M. (2008). Mentoring beginning primary teachers for exemplary teaching practices. *Teaching and Teacher Education, 24,* 684–702.

Spendlove, D., Howes, A., & Wake, G. (2010). Partnerships in pedagogy: refocusing of classroom lenses. *European Journal of Teacher Education, 33*(1), 65–77. https://doi.org/10.1080/02619760903414116.

Srivastava, P., & Hopwood, N. (2009). A practical iterative framework for qualitative data analysis. *International Journal of Qualitative Methods, 8*(1), 76–84.

Teacher Education Ministerial Advisory Group [TEMAG]. (2014). *Action now: Classroom ready teachers.* Retrieved from https://www.studentsfirst.gov.au/teacher-education-ministerial-advisory-group.

Tracy, S. (2013). *Qualitative research methods: Collecting evidence, crafting analysis, communicating impact.* Chichester, UK: Wiley-Blackwell.

Turner, B., Abercrombie, N., & Hill, S. (2006). *The Penguin dictionary of sociology.* London, United Kingdom: Penguin.

Uusimaki, L. (2013). Empowering pre-service teacher supervisors' perspectives: A relational-cultural approach towards mentoring. *Australian Journal of Teacher Education, 38*(7), 45–58.

van Velzen, C., Volman, M., Brekelmans, M., & White, S. (2012). Guided work-based learning: Sharing practical teaching knowledge with student teachers. *Teaching and Teacher Education, 28,* 229–239. https://doi.org/10.1016/j.tate.2011.09.011.

Walkington, J. (2007). Improving partnerships between schools and universities: Professional learning with benefits beyond preservice teacher education. *Teacher Development, 11*(3), 277–294.

White, E. (2014). Being a teacher and a teacher educator: Developing a new identity? *Professional Development in Education, 40*(3), 436–449.

Author Biographies

Amanda Isaac began her career teaching in primary schools but has worked in initial teacher education for over 15 years. She is currently based at the Lismore campus of Southern Cross University. The majority of her work is in the area of professional experience, working with pre-service teachers and schools to make links between the theoretical and practical aspects of initial teacher education. She is new to research and has a particular interest in the experiences and perceptions of supervising teachers.

Suzanne Hudson (PhD) has been involved in teaching and teacher education for over 35 years. Currently the Director of Professional Experience across the three campuses of Southern Cross University, Sue has held various leadership roles in the tertiary sector. From 2008 to 2012, Sue was the project leader for a large Australian Federal Government grant titled "Teacher Education Done Differently" (TEDD) that integrated school-based learning experiences into the Bachelor of Education (Primary) programme at QUT's Caboolture campus. The TEDD project team was recognised with an Australian Award for University Teaching (AAUT) Citation in 2012 and an award the following year (2013) for Programs that Enhance Student Learning. Sue is the co-developer of the Mentoring for Effective Teaching (MET) programme that develops the skills and practices of mentor teachers. MET has been successfully delivered across Australia and in the USA, Hong Kong and the Philippines. Although Sue has a range of research interests, university-school partnerships, professional experience, innovative approaches to teacher education, and induction and mentoring are a focus for Sue's research.

Chapter 5
Listening to Mentor Teachers' Voices in Uncertain Times

Ruth Radford, Kerry Howells and John Williamson

Abstract One characteristic of the uncertain times in teacher education is the complexity involved in operationalising the various standards and policy documents when little attention is given to how best to use the time in school-based practicum so that it is both educative and purposeful. This is a "wicked problem" to which various theories and literature miss the mark if not informed by those at the coalface. We argue that to navigate this complex terrain we need to include the voice of the mentor teacher. Up to this point, there has been a global silence on the crucial importance of this voice. Yet, in many instances, the mentor teachers develop considerable expertise and professional judgements about how to produce confident, capable, resilient and reflective novice teachers. This voice needs to be recognised and listened to in, not only informing policy and articulating standards but in bridging the gap between policy and practice. Our research investigated how mentor teachers, working within a program where pre-service teachers had significant amounts of practicum time, and in a context of high Education Needs Index schools, understood teaching pre-service teachers to teach. Through qualitative inquiry using the method of a case study, this chapter investigates the views of 30 mentor teachers across 12 schools (both primary and secondary). The broad themes from our data analysis are relationships, reciprocity, responsibility and reflection. We argue that these aspects add a rich and crucial dimension to standard statements and pedagogy around school-based mentoring.

R. Radford (✉) · K. Howells · J. Williamson
University of Tasmania, Hobart, TAS, Australia
e-mail: Ruth.Radford@utas.edu.au

K. Howells
e-mail: Kerry.Howells@utas.edu.au

J. Williamson
e-mail: John.Williamson@utas.edu.au

© Springer Nature Singapore Pte Ltd. 2018
D. Heck and A. Ambrosetti (eds.), *Teacher Education In and For Uncertain Times*,
https://doi.org/10.1007/978-981-10-8648-9_5

Keywords Relationships · Mentoring · Intentionality · Teachers' voice ·
Pre-service teacher education

Introduction

These are uncertain times for teacher education. In this chapter, we examine the role
of school-based mentor teachers in initial teacher education and the interpretation
of teaching standards as a guide to action. We believe that teachers in schools, who
take on the role of mentoring pre-service teachers, have the potential to provide
significant guidance to policy and practices around teacher education. We agree with
scholars who have noted that their voices are not given sufficient prominence in
teacher education research or policy (Cochran-Smith & Zeichner, 2010; Hagger &
McIntyre, 2006; Yendol-Hoppey, Jacobs, & Dana, 2009).

Much teacher education research conveys a negative message about pre-service
teachers' experience in schools. This time has been described as a "wicked problem"
(Southgate, Reynolds, & Howley, 2013) and a "vexed issue" (Le Cornu, 2016). Scholars explain that teachers who mentor pre-service teachers primarily understand their
role as renters of a "safe site" (Hobson, Ashby, Malderez, & Tomlinson, 2009), where
the pre-service teachers are "guests" in the classrooms (Valencia, Martin, Place, &
Grossman, 2009) and keeping the peace and being polite becomes more important
than teaching about teaching (Cain, 2009). Beliefs that teaching is "caught rather
than taught" prevail (Southgate et al., 2013). When mentor teachers see their role as
merely a "giver of space" for practice, it is likely that they give little thought to their
responsibility as a teacher of teaching. Certainly, there is a lack of clarity about the
mentor teacher role (Hamel & Jaasko-Fisher, 2011). They generally appear to interpret their role as nurturers (Hennissen, Crasborn, Brouwer, Korthagen, & Bergen,
2011) providing emotional support rather than focus on pedagogy. Yet research on
the role of mentor teachers argues that teachers taking on the mentoring role should
understand that they are school-based teacher educators (Feiman-Nemser, 1998)
responsible for "an intentional set of experiences and learning" (Darling-Hammond
& Lieberman, 2012, p. 162).

Educative Mentoring

Most countries have standards that guide best practice at different stages of teaching.
In the Australian context, these are the Australian Professional Standards for Teachers (AITSL, 2011). When Australian teachers reach the most experienced or "lead
teacher" level, they are expected to be "skilled in mentoring". To do this, they lead
processes and initiatives; support and assist colleagues; demonstrate, model, initiate
collaborative relationships and implement professional dialogue (AITSL, 2011). As
with all standards documents, it is the interpretation within educational communi-

ties that gives meaning to these broad statements. Nevertheless, these teachers are described as highly sophisticated in their knowledge, understanding and skills. They are educative mentors (Feiman-Nemser, 1998). Here, we investigate the literature to see what educative mentoring involves as a basis for situating our data that analyses how a group of mentor teachers understood teaching pre-service teachers to teach.

Educative mentoring focuses on student learning and is reform-minded (Wang & Odell, 2006) and has been variously described as constructivist, learner centred, responsive and teaching for understanding (Cohen, McLaughlin, & Talbert, 1993). It is teaching that aims to make learning visible and holds a commitment to assist all students to succeed (Hattie, 2012). Hence, teachers must "suspend habitual notions that presume sameness" (Ball & Cohen, 1999, p. 9) and base their teaching on a deep understanding of diversity. This is demanding teaching and must be learned in practice because "teaching occurs in particulars—particular students interacting with particular teachers over particular ideas in particular circumstances" (Ball & Cohen, 1999, p. 10).

In seeking to establish approaches to mentoring practice that are educative, the more expert educator must not only take on responsibility for an intentional set of experiences but also a responsibility for relationships. This means maintaining an understanding of how relationships are inextricably connected with learning (Hattie, 2012). Considering responsibility for relationships invites us to consider notions of interconnectedness, the ways relationships support and foster a sense of responsibility for the other. Underpinning the idea of interconnectedness is the argument that our sense of self, our developing mind, and our confident practice is "a choreography of co-action" (Gergen, 2009, p. 137).

Mentored learning to teach means having a deep sense of the value of situated classroom learning (Brown, Collins, & Duguid, 1989; Lave & Wenger, 1991). The mentor teacher encourages the "legitimate peripheral participation" (Lave & Wenger, 1991) of the novice in the authentic tasks of teaching (Ball & Cohen, 1999). Teaching performance is assisted with consciously chosen tasks that are within reach of the novice because readiness and the "zone of proximal development" (Vygotsky, 1978, p. 86) or level of potential development has been assessed. This process is described as "scaffolding". As the mentor teacher provides opportunities for assisted performance, it is the meaningful dialogue, where the "expert's" thinking is made visible (Collins, Brown, & Newman, 1989), that builds the pre-service teacher's capacity to interpret or read the students and make meaning of situations and the repercussions of decisions.

Educative mentoring encourages pre-service teachers to be reflective practitioners. Donald Schön (1983, 1987) describes two categories of reflection. The first is what Schön called reflection-in-action (1983, p. 69) and this is "the most complex and demanding kind of reflection … [that] develops only as a consequence of considerable experience (Hatton & Smith, 1995, p. 44). This experience builds through what Schön called reflection-on-action. Hence, the usefulness of Hatton and Smith's succinct definition of reflection as "deliberate thinking about action with a view to its improvement" (Hatton & Smith, 1995, p. 40).

Taking all of this into account our conceptual framework is based on the notion that school-based teacher educators must understand their role as educative (Dewey, 1938; Feiman-Nemser, 1998, 2012) and take responsibility for being teachers of teaching. This means mentoring is more than emotional support, technical advice and an opportunity for adjustment to the school context (Little, 1990). Being a school-based teacher educator means taking responsibility for a purposeful focus on student learning (Feiman-Nemser, 1998); relationships where the pre-service teacher is thought of as a reciprocal learner (Ambrosetti, 2014; van Ginkel, Verloop, & Denessen, 2016); provision of an authentic situated experience (Lave & Wenger, 1991) with a gradual release of teaching responsibility (Feiman-Nemser, 2012); and finally, an inquiry and questioning stance to practice that understands teaching as a career long learning journey (Cochran-Smith & Lytle, 2001; Evelein & Korthagen, 2015).

We build too on literature that argues for much greater involvement, in policy and research, by mentor teachers. Cochran-Smith and Paris (1995) argue, "mentoring has the greatest potential to contribute to reform in teacher education" (p. 182) but only if the concept is reconceptualised. Mentoring must be based on an epistemology that "includes teachers' ways of knowing and acting about teaching" (Cochran-Smith & Paris, 1995, p. 184). In 2007 Yendol-Hoppey noted that there was little that reveals "how mentor teachers, conceptualised as school based-teacher educators, shape and conduct their work with student teachers" (p. 670). In these uncertain times, giving significance to the expertise of mentor teachers is critical because there is substantial acknowledgement that ultimately teaching is learned in and from practice (Ball & Cohen, 1999; Hammerness, Darling-Hammond, Grossman, Rust, & Shulman, 2005).

There is a sense in which the literature on educative mentoring is aspirational. While there are examples of novices' deep learning in schools (Feiman-Nemser, 2012; Feiman-Nemser & Beasley, 2007), using school-based time well is challenging. This is a core area of uncertainty in initial teacher education. The AITSL standards map the territory. However, to enhance and improve the time pre-service teachers spend in schools, an important contribution will be the insights from mentor teachers. To investigate these insights, we asked: How did the teachers, who took on the mentor teacher role in the five-year Partnerships in Teaching Excellence program, understand teaching pre-service teachers to teach?

Context

The Partnerships in Teaching Excellence program were a partnership between the University of Tasmania and the Tasmanian Education Department (Allen, Howells, & Radford, 2013). The program ran for five years and involved 14 schools: five secondary schools (grades 7–10), eight primary schools (grades K-6) and one rural District school (grades K-10). The program selected a number of pre-service teachers in the final year of their undergraduate or postgraduate education degree for an opportunity to spend additional time in high Education Needs Index (ENI) schools.

This amounted to around 40 additional days, a significant increase on the normal time given to pre-service teachers in schools, which is generally around 60 days. The pre-service teachers were allocated, usually in small groups, to one of the 14 schools where selected teachers worked as mentors. In this program, mentor teachers also took a prominent role as assessors when working with the university professional experience assessor. Hence, the Partnerships in Teaching Excellence program were an opportunity to investigate, from the mentor teachers' viewpoints, what was involved in teaching about teaching in school settings.

Research Design

Participants and Data Collection

A case study approach was selected for this research. A case study was chosen for its capacity to capture the depth and complexity of the "lived reality" (Glesne & Peshkin, 1992; Stake, 2000) of the teachers' experience. Following ethics approval, 78 mentor teachers from the 14 schools were invited to participate. Thirty teachers volunteered for the project.

To research the participants' understanding about teaching pre-service teachers to teach, semi-structured interviews were chosen as the method of data collection. Glesne and Peshkin (1992) write that "the interview can be the sole basis of study" (p. 64), particularly when, as was relevant to this case study, the purpose of the research is to describe the participants' perspective on events. The interview questions were developed, trialled and revised. The completed set of questions provided a guided format that was followed flexibly with all participants. The digital recordings were professionally transcribed and original names were turned into pseudonyms or deleted. Participants were sent a copy of their interview for member checking.

In the interviews, the participants were asked what pre-service teachers should be learning while they were in schools and how they, as mentor teachers, taught this. The questions sought to explore their values and beliefs as well as their knowledge and capabilities in mentoring pre-service teachers.

Data Analysis

An inductive data analysis approach was used. This involved the analysis of the 30 interview texts to search for patterns and themes. The inductive analysis moved from reading the interview transcripts to coding "chunks of text" that provided general answers to our research question. The inductive data analysis involved reading and re-reading the coded texts. The text sections that referred to the emerging themes were extracted, additional research questions were posed, and the text sections were recoded. Through a recursive and iterative process (Bazeley, 2014) categories were identified within the themes that interpreted how the teachers in this study understood teaching their pre-service teachers to teach. NVivo (Version 10) was used to assist with management of the data.

Findings

Our research provides substantial insight into what a sample of school-based teacher educators believed to be the important aspects of the mentoring role with pre-service teachers. Coding of data revealed four broad intricately interconnected themes: relationships, reciprocity, responsibility and reflection. The interconnecting idea across the themes is taking responsibility for relationships or "relational responsibility" (Gergen, 2009). This concept encompasses the recognition of our connectedness with and responsibility for the other. Mentor teachers who took a proactive and explicit stance towards their responsibility for the "other" also appeared to understand more consciously their responsibility for teaching pre-service teachers to teach.

Relationships

The concept of relationships encompasses the felt connection between the mentor teacher and pre-service teacher. For most of these participants, this was "the most important thing". The concept of relationships includes notions of support and nurturing that the mentor teacher typically feels for the novice. These participants understood that there were many aspects to this relationship: their own confidence as teachers and a positive orientation to being a teacher; their capacity to manage irritations and potential resentments around the extra time involved and tensions in sharing their classroom with another adult; knowing their pre-service teacher well, particularly as a learner; building trust for honest conversations and finally the importance of collegial relationships in the life of a school.

Here, we emphasise being aware of the pre-service teacher as a learner and acknowledging attributes common to novices learning to teach. For instance, understanding their ability to read the classroom as a teacher did not happen automatically. Sometimes the pre-service teachers "don't know what to look for" (Judy) and many participants described assisting the pre-service teachers to "notice and understand" (Patricia) what was happening in the complex world of classrooms. They understood that it was often "hard to think beyond what you are teaching at that moment" (Carmel). The long history of time spent as students in classrooms was also problematic. "Their default mode is to teach how they were taught" (Susan), and this was "not always the best way" (Alan).

Judging readiness and progress over time was important for maintaining the relationship. This sometimes meant reassessing their expectations and "take a few steps backwards, starting at a lower level rather than where we were expecting to" (Laura) or empathizing with the complexity of what learning to teach entailed because a novice's "short term memory's so taken up with the moment of, what am I going to do next and how can I teach this, they may miss it" (Kristina). The mentor teachers judged progress by looking for examples of confidence, as Alan explained, "If they are finding it difficult to take a small group, I don't want to have them under pressure to take the whole class".

The mentors reported that this relationship was the foundation for all the conversations that would take place over the year. A good relationship meant you could be honest and frank, "in order to have that conversation you need to know that you're not being judged and that the feedback is to help with improving their practice" (Alan). A trusting relationship meant the pre-service teacher felt safe to ask questions, particularly questions about their mentor teacher's practice. This is what most participants considered as the key outcome of a trusting relationship between themselves and their pre-service teacher. They built what Claire called "working trust" by sharing "a bit of yourself" (Charles). They acknowledged their teaching "mistakes" and struggles because "struggling is a really big thing to share" (Elizabeth). These teachers knew that pre-service teachers were bound to make mistakes. In making explicit their own mistakes the mentor teachers intentionally made themselves vulnerable and demonstrated their belief that you are never finished with learning to teach.

Reciprocity

Reciprocity between mentor teachers and pre-service teachers describes a sense of mutuality or partnership that develops between some mentors and pre-service teachers. Most commonly this is expressed through mutual appreciation of the other's contribution. These participants made explicit that they valued working with a pre-service teacher. Some mentor teachers talked about the dangers of "trundling along" and being "set in your ways" and described their appreciation for being given a "bit of a slap" and becoming "revitalised", "mindful", and "a better teacher" who was "enjoying it more" all because of their relationship with their pre-service teacher.

Several mentor teachers expressed appreciation, as Carmel did, at having "someone to bounce my ideas off, who could see it. It wasn't just someone coming in, it was someone *in* there". John also noted the benefit of another adult regularly in his classroom, "I learned so much about how my class actually operated". Other mentor teachers valued the subject expertise the pre-service teachers brought into planning. "It was our first year of the Australian Curriculum so she actually helped us" (Carmel). Still, others commented on the pleasure they had from seeing growth over the year. Laura commented on the satisfaction of seeing "her blossom and really come into herself", and for Claire, seeing "real growth", was "really powerful".

Moving beyond the rhetoric of appreciation, to being mutual learners about learning and teaching, appeared to be a more complex matter. Our data suggest that this sense of mutuality in the relationship did not come about automatically. Many participants appeared to take their relationship for granted as a necessary component of having a pre-service teacher in their classroom. Taking responsibility for the relationship, on the other hand, encouraged the mentor teachers to see, as Tess explained, that they were working with someone who was "more like your equal. They were able to offer you something as well it wasn't just going to be a one-way relationship".

Our data revealed that these participants varied in the extent to which they established a mutual learning relationship with their pre-service teacher. For some mentor teachers, a number of perceptions about learning to teach appeared to form barriers to partnership. One such belief was about initiative. Some participants believed that it was the pre-service teacher's responsibility to show initiative. Adrienne explained, "You rely on the student you have … you really rely on them telling you what they want out of it. … they have to be fairly proactive". Furthermore, because "you can't teach initiative" (Katrina) no responsibility could be taken for this aspect of the relationship. For others, their perceptions about learning to teach seemed to place limits on the extent to which they developed a sense of interconnectedness with their pre-service teacher. Some believed pre-service teachers needed to come with "a quality", and that "teaching is an art and in some ways … it can't be taught" (Katrina). Hence some participants, while they provided opportunities for learning to teach and emotional support, did not take responsibility for a relationship that built a sense of mutual learning about teaching with their pre-service teacher.

Other mentor teachers took more responsibility for this relationship. They focused on the other "as someone who really wants to learn and how can I best support them to do that" (Barbara). As Claire explained:

> I guess not having that hubris of practice. It's almost willing to put ego aside and just be open to someone who's learning, who will ask questions that unsettle you without realizing that that's what they're doing.

Believing in their pre-service teacher's capacity to learn meant these participants were oriented to interconnectedness. Stephanie and other mentor teachers emphasised that learning to teach, "doesn't come naturally", and "they don't know what they don't know" (Judy, Kristina, Laura). This view encouraged participants to take responsibility for a relationship with a learner. They described a partnership in the classroom where "we're almost learning alongside each other" (Kristina). Furthermore, several participants used inclusive language particularly turning the "I" in the story of the classroom to "we". Barbara described how, "*We* would sit together in our spare time and look at those bigger ideas and how *we* could pull that into our teaching and learning practice … we would just basically *co-plan*." Kristina, however, described a conscious and purposeful use of the pronoun "we":

You need to have the demeanour that you're not a know-all and that you don't want to make them feel inferior. ... you're as much a learner as they are. Sometimes I'll put, now how could we have improved that, 'we', using that 'we'. ... That didn't go so well. I wonder what was wrong with our planning with that, how can we improve that?

Responsibility

Mentor teachers talked about feeling responsible, committed and accountable for their pre-service teachers' learning to teach. The concept of responsibility includes a sense of intentionality about what pre-service teachers should learn and how their learning should be supported and responsibly assessed. This sense of intentionality grows out of taking responsibility for the relationship.

These mentors emphasised a number of priorities as part of their responsibility for their pre-service teachers' learning to teach. They all the stressed that their pre-service teachers must get to know their students well because it was on relationships that "all learning is hinged" (Kristina). Building these relationships was often hard work and while some participants seemed to believe this should come "naturally", others realised that "not everybody comes into teaching with the ability to build relationships straight up" (Charles). Other priorities included understanding the importance of routines in the classroom; planning for teaching; modelling various aspects of teaching; providing opportunities for practice and consciously sequencing the challenges. Alan called this approach "gradual release helping". Claire and other mentor teachers talked about scaffolding or thinking about "how you will get them to a point". These participants also emphasised making time for talk about teaching and acknowledged the responsibility involved in making their final assessments, where it "would come back to all of that evidence that I've collected along the way" (Barbara).

Not all the participants were consciously intentional about how the pre-service teachers used their classroom time. Examining the data revealed a continuum best captured by two uses of the metaphor "osmosis". At one end, a mentor teacher commented that the pre-service teachers "learnt more just by osmosis from—just hanging out with us" (Miles). This was contrasted by Stephanie's observation that "It's not osmosis". For instance, when mentor teachers were intentional about what they were modelling, they provided a focus for observation. Kristina emphasised that "I don't just leave a student to just sit and look ... I'll be saying when I'm taking this lesson this is what I want you to look at". They modelled such things as using your voice; setting up and running group rotations; giving instructions and explanations; making transitions between activities; ways to build relationships; collecting evidence on student progress and making assessments. For some mentor teachers, this meant realising:

I had to be the teacher of the student teacher more ... I had to model a lot more. I had to show her more of how to teach rather than expecting her to go and plan a lesson and go and do it. (Laura)

Reflection

Reflection was a concept used by most of the mentor teachers, and this strongly relates to the other themes. Developing the capacity to reflect on relationships was seen as essential to taking greater responsibility and teaching more intentionally.

First, the mentors used the concept when talking about the need to think about their own teaching. "If you've got people observing, then you need to make sure that you can reflect and say, did that work so well, do I need to change things?" (Carmel). Hence, many of the mentor teachers described "unpacking" their practice, becoming more "conscious", and growing "through having to be really explicit about what I was doing and why" (Steve).

Second, they reflected on their pre-service teacher's practice and responses to classroom situations. Sometimes this meant being surprised by what they themselves took for granted such as Carmel's description of when the children were "just getting their lunchboxes, it turned into quite a shemozzle, and then we both sat back and went, ah!" Taking responsibility for the relationship with the novice, meant helping them notice, understand and act on their experience, even uncomfortable ones, while at the same time "keeping that confidence up" (Jackie).

Third, they talked about assisting their pre-service teachers to be reflective. Having a deeper understanding about what they were doing meant these participants were able to demonstrate how to think and talk about the details of the classroom. Furthermore, taking relational responsibility facilitated co-action as the basis for shared meaning-making and co-thinking. For instance, they talked through their plans, guiding their pre-service teachers' thinking through how the students' interests will be engaged, timing, instructions, transitions and catering for specific students. Several participants used this reflection-for-action to encourage their pre-service teachers to justify, "Why would you do it that way? ... I want to know what the reasons are behind it" (John).

Questioning became significant for reflective feedback conversations. Questioning pushed the pre-service teachers to be the ones deepening their thinking through describing, explaining, justifying, analysing and thinking forward to action. Many mentor teachers described learning to "hang back" because "you have to just learn to let her speak and you just come up with the right question at the right time. You don't always get it right. ... You almost have to bite your tongue sometimes!" (Marcus). Posing questions was important because, as Barbara explained, "I wanted her to do the thinking herself".

Our data show these participants focused much of their reflective talk on their students' learning. Many participants commented on the challenge for pre-service teachers of "the bigger learning ... going from that focusing on task to thinking about the learning and moving students forward" (Claire). For Claire, it was "imperative to know the children as learners" in order to think reflectively before, during and following teaching. As Kristina explained this meant considering, "what learning outcomes do I want to achieve?" Thinking about learning intentions provided a foundation for thinking about evidence of the children's progress. Thinking about progress provided the basis for reflective conversations that pushed pre-service teachers to be specific and constantly invited thoughts about improving practice:

> How did that student go with that task? What did they get out of it? What will we do next time? How will we make sure? What sort of formative assessment tools do we have in place to make sure that they're learning? (Marcus).

Discussion and Conclusion: From Policy to Practice

This study demonstrates the vital role that the voice of the mentor teacher can play in articulating the practical dimensions of policy. Listening to what mentor teachers say about what is important in teaching pre-service teachers to teach will continue to be a crucial activity as we navigate these uncertain times in initial teacher education. Practical wisdom captured by these mentor teachers in the domains of relationships, reciprocity, responsibility and reflection heralds the potential of listening to the mentor voice providing important insights on how we are to achieve the aspirations of policy framed as national teaching and program standards.

The AITSL Lead teacher standards provide a map that seeks to answer what is involved in educating quality teachers. These standards are an extrapolation from the description of the proficient teacher and appear to suggest that expert teachers are inevitably successful mentor teachers. This assumption is strongly contested (Ambrosetti, 2014; Bullough Jr, 2005; Hobson et al., 2009; Le Cornu, 2012). The most pertinent section of the standards indicates that the Lead teacher will "Initiate collaborative relationships ... to provide quality opportunities and placements for pre-service teachers" (AITSL, 2011 Descriptor 6.2). Our study indicates that what is involved in meeting this standard, and the "relational capacities" that are involved (Le Cornu, 2015, p. 14), is much more complex than is implied by the standard. Furthermore, many participants stressed that being an educative mentor teacher or school-based teacher educator is "a full role in itself" (Adrienne).

Listening to the voices of these mentor teachers reveals several important implications for translating the standards map into practice. First, these participants underline the importance of the layers of relationships that are critical for learning to teach. This study suggests that what is critical is that mentor teachers understand that their pre-service teacher is an adult learner and that they build this relationship intentionally, sustaining it with conscious reflection on empathy and sensitivity.

Second, listening to these mentor teachers provides insights about moving along what can be thought of as a continuum of practice. Those who perceive learning to teach as something "caught" while "hanging about" in classrooms seriously underestimate what there is to learn about teaching. Interpreting this continuum assists mentor teachers to understand themselves as mutual learners who together construct meaning around specific children, situations and decisions. This means they develop a theory of learning to teach that goes beyond hoping for osmosis.

Third, placing pre-service teachers for more time in schools will not of itself necessarily mean that teachers will see themselves as a teacher of teaching. Some of our participants were less intentional, while others deliberately took the opportunity of school and classroom situations for "knitting everything together" (Claire). There needs to be respectful guidance and support for teachers undertaking this role. Relational responsibility and mutual learning between university staff and school leaders with the teachers who assume the mentor teacher role is necessary to support deliberate, intentional and responsible practice. Finally, the data suggest that central to assisting mentor teachers in becoming a mutual learner with their pre-service teacher will be a shared focus on ongoing, reflective conversations about teaching diverse learners, and, how learning progress is determined through the interpretation of evidence.

These implications lead us to make three recommendations. First that a set of standards be developed that respects that being a mentor teacher is a full role in itself. Second, professional learning support for mentor teachers be provided in a concurrent form and explicitly, and respectfully, address where, as learners, they are on the continuum towards mutuality. Third, that supporting policy documents and initial teaching education curriculum take greater responsibility for the place of relationships in learning to teach.

In these uncertain times, the human world of meaning-making is not easily controlled "by discourses of regulation and accountability" (Le Cornu, 2016, p. 5). What we have in this study are teachers acknowledging the other as a learner about teaching; making themselves vulnerable as learners as they work as co-planners, co-teachers and co-assessors. In this mutually respectful way, they learn together how to teach a specific group of children well, questioning their practice as they go. This joint work makes the learning authentic and valuable to both expert and novice. At the core are teachers working in an intentional and educative way where they take responsibility for relationships and the reflective process. This is very sophisticated work, and mentor teachers also need to be alert to what they are learning about being a teacher of teaching. Those of us outside schools must position ourselves better so that we are learning with them and from them.

References

Allen, J. M., Howells, K., & Radford, R. (2013). A 'partnership in teaching excellence': Ways in which one school–university partnership has fostered teacher development. *Asia-Pacific Journal of Teacher Education, 41*(1), 99–110.

Ambrosetti, A. (2014). Are you ready to be a mentor? Preparing teachers for mentoring pre-service teachers. *Australian Journal of Teacher Education, 39*(6), 30–42.

Australian Institute for Teaching and School Leadership (AITSL). (2011). *National professional standards for teachers.* Canberra: Ministerial Council for Education Early Childhood Development and Youth Affairs.

Ball, D. L., & Cohen, D. K. (1999). Developing practice, developing practitioners: Toward a practice-based theory of professional education. In L. Darling-Hammond & G. Sykes (Eds.), *Teaching as the learning profession: Handbook of policy and practice* (pp. 3–32). San Francisco, CA: Jossey-Bass.

Bazeley, P. (2014). *Qualitative data analysis: Practical strategies.* London: Sage.

Brown, J. S., Collins, A., & Duguid, P. (1989). Situated cognition and the culture of learning. *Educational Researcher, 18*(1), 32–42.

Bullough, R. V., Jr. (2005). Being and becoming a mentor: School-based teacher educators and teacher educator identity. *Teaching and Teacher Education, 21*(2), 143–155.

Cain, T. (2009). Mentoring trainee teachers: How can mentors use research? *Mentoring & Tutoring: Partnership in Learning, 17*(1), 53–66.

Cochran-Smith, M., & Lytle, S. L. (2001). Beyond certainty: Taking an inquiry stance on practice. In A. Lieberman & L. Miller (Eds.), *Teachers caught in the action: Professional development that matters* (pp. 45–58). New York: Teachers College Press.

Cochran-Smith, M., & Paris, C. L. (1995). Mentor and mentoring: Did Homer have it right? In J. Smyth (Ed.), *Critical discourses on teacher development* (pp. 181–202). London: Cassell.

Cochran-Smith, M., & Zeichner, K. M. (Eds.). (2010). *Studying teacher education: The report of the AERA panel on research and teacher education.* New York: Routledge.

Cohen, D. K., McLaughlin, M. W., & Talbert, J. E. (1993). *Teaching for understanding: Challenges, for practice, research, and policy.* New York: Jossey-Bass.

Collins, A., Brown, J. S., & Newman, S. E. (1989). Cognitive apprenticeship: Teaching the crafts of reading, writing, and mathematics. In L. B. Resnick (Ed.), *Knowing, learning, and instruction: Essays in honor of Robert Glaser* (pp. 453–494). Hillsdale, NJ: Lawrence Erlbaum Associates.

Darling-Hammond, L., & Lieberman, A. (2012). *Teacher education around the world: Changing policies and practices.* London: Routledge.

Dewey, J. (1938). *Experience and education.* New York, NY: Free Press.

Evelein, F. G., & Korthagen, F. (2015). *Practicing core reflection: Activities and lessons for teaching and learning from within.* New York, NY: Routledge.

Feiman-Nemser, S. (1998). Teachers as teacher educators. *European Journal of Teacher Education, 21*(1), 63–74.

Feiman-Nemser, S. (2012). *Teachers as learners.* Cambridge, MA: Harvard Education Press.

Feiman-Nemser, S., & Beasley, K. (2007). Discovering and sharing knowledge: Inventing a new role for cooperating teachers. In D. Carroll, H. Featherstone, J. Featherstone, S. Feiman-Nemser, & D. Roosevelt (Eds.), *Transforming teacher education: Reflections from the field* (pp. 139–160). Cambridge, MA: Harvard Education Press.

Gergen, K. J. (2009). *Relational being: Beyond self and community.* New York, NY: Oxford University Press.

Glesne, C., & Peshkin, A. (1992). *Becoming qualitative researchers: An introduction.* White Plains, NY: Longman.

Hagger, H., & McIntyre, D. (2006). *Learning teaching from teachers: Realising the potential of school-based teacher education.* Maidenhead, Berks: McGraw-Hill International.

Hamel, F. L., & Jaasko-Fisher, H. A. (2011). Hidden labor in the mentoring of pre-service teachers: Notes from a mentor advisory council. *Teaching and Teacher Education, 27,* 434–442.

Hammerness, K., Darling-Hammond, L., Grossman, P., Rust, F., & Shulman, L. S. (2005). The design of teacher education programs. In L. Darling-Hammond & J. Bransford (Eds.), *Preparing teachers for a changing world: What teachers should learn and be able to do* (pp. 390–441). San Francisco, CA: Jossey-Bass.

Hattie, J. (2012). *Visible learning for teachers: Maximizing impact on learning.* London: Routledge.

Hatton, N., & Smith, D. (1995). Reflection in teacher education: Towards definition and implementation. *Teaching and Teacher Education, 11*(1), 33–49.

Hennissen, P., Crasborn, F., Brouwer, N., Korthagen, F., & Bergen, T. (2011). Clarifying pre-service teacher perceptions of mentor teachers' developing use of mentoring skills. *Teaching and Teacher Education, 27*(6), 1049–1058.

Hobson, A. J., Ashby, P., Malderez, A., & Tomlinson, P. D. (2009). Mentoring beginning teachers: What we know and what we don't. *Teaching and Teacher Education, 25*(1), 207–216.

Lave, J., & Wenger, E. (1991). *Situated learning: Legitimate peripheral participation.* Cambridge: Cambridge University Press.

Le Cornu, R. (2012). School co-ordinators: Leaders of learning in professional experience. *Australian Journal of Teacher Education, 37*(3), 18–33.

Le Cornu, R. (2015). *Key components of effective professional experience in initial teacher education in Australia*. Melbourne: Australian Institute for Teaching and School Leadership.

Le Cornu, R. (2016). Professional experience: Learning from the past to build the future. *Asia-Pacific Journal of Teacher Education, 44*(1), 80–101.

Little, J. W. (1990). The mentor phenomenon and the social organization of teaching. *Review of Research in Education, 16,* 297–351.

Schön, D. A. (1983). *The reflective practitioner: How professionals think in action*. New York, NY: Basic Books.

Schön, D. A. (1987). *Educating the reflective practitioner: Toward a new design for teaching and learning in the professions*. San Francisco, CA: Jossey-Bass.

Southgate, E., Reynolds, R., & Howley, P. (2013). Professional experience as a wicked problem in initial teacher education. *Teaching and Teacher Education, 31,* 13–22.

Stake, R. (2000). Case studies. In N. K. Denzin & Y. S. Lincoln (Eds.), *The Sage handbook of qualitative research* (2nd ed., pp. 435–454). Thousand Oaks, CA: Sage.

Valencia, S. W., Martin, S. D., Place, N. A., & Grossman, P. (2009). Complex interactions in student teaching: Lost opportunities for learning. *Journal of Teacher Education, 60*(3), 304–322.

van Ginkel, G., Verloop, N., & Denessen, E. (2016). Why mentor? Linking mentor teachers' motivations to their mentoring conceptions. *Teachers and Teaching, 22*(1), 101–116.

Vygotsky, L. S. (1978). *Mind in society: The development of higher psychological processes* (M. Cole, Trans.). Cambridge, MA: Harvard University Press.

Wang, J., & Odell, S. J. (2006). An alternative conception of mentor–novice relationships: Learning to teach in reform-minded ways as a context. *Teaching and Teacher Education, 23*(4), 473–489.

Yendol-Hoppey, D. (2007). Mentor teachers' work with prospective teachers in a newly formed professional development school: Two illustrations. *Teachers College Record, 109*(3), 669–698.

Yendol-Hoppey, D., Jacobs, J., & Dana, N. F. (2009). Critical concepts of mentoring in an urban context. *The New Educator, 5,* 25–44.

Author Biographies

Ruth Radford is a Ph.D. candidate in the School of Education, University of Tasmania. She has worked in secondary school teaching, Initial Teacher Education teaching, and curriculum and professional learning roles in the Tasmanian Department of Education. From 2009 to 2013, she was the Department's manager of the Partnerships in Teaching Excellence project. This project placed selected pre-service students in a number of high Educational Needs Index (ENI) Tasmanian schools for a year concurrent with the final year of their education degree. At the end of 2013, she retired as Principal Education Officer in the Department to pursue her research into how teachers, mentoring pre-service teachers, understand teaching about teaching.

Kerry Howells is an academic and teacher educator in the Faculty of Education at the University of Tasmania, where she teaches in the areas of professional studies, teacher leadership and gratitude in education. She was the university coordinator of the Partnership in Teaching Excellence project. Her research spans the last two decades of critical inquiry into the role of gratitude in education, with a particular focus on teacher identity and teacher integrity. She has investigated this approach in a range of contexts, including pre-service teacher education, school leadership, high school teaching, early childhood education and elite sport. She has presented her research and approach to teaching and learning through gratitude in invited presentations at numerous universities, schools and other contexts across five continents.

John Williamson is Professor Emeritus in the School of Education at the University of Tasmania. He has published widely in the areas of teachers' work lives, teacher education and classroom pedagogy. Currently, he is researching the range of selection criteria into Initial Teacher Education in Australia, how a number of Tasmanian High Schools are implementing the Government policy of extending to year 11 and year 12, and how accountability is perceived by teachers in nine countries. He is a member of several national committees including the Teacher Education Expert Standing Committee (TEESC) of AITSL, the National Teacher Data Workforce Strategy group and the AITSL Teaching Performance Assessment Grant programme Steering Committee.

Chapter 6
Building Resilience in Times of Uncertainty and Complexity: Teacher Educator Perceptions of Pre-service Teacher Resilience

Caroline Mansfield, Lisa Papatraianou, Sharon McDonough and Laura King

Abstract An emphasis on teacher quality in Australia has resulted in many changes in teacher education including a recent emphasis on non-academic capabilities (such as resilience) of prospective teachers. Reporting data obtained through an online survey of 73 teacher educators, this chapter presents their views about pre-service teacher resilience and the role of teacher educators and education programs in promoting resilience for pre-service teachers. Findings illustrate the multiple contexts important in the development of teacher resilience and how resilience can be demonstrated during the pre-service years. Barriers and supports for embedding resilience in teacher education programs are discussed. We argue that in times of uncertainty and complexity in teacher education, resilience is critical for sustained effectiveness and growth.

Keywords Teacher education · Teacher resilience · Non-academic capabilities, context

C. Mansfield (✉) · L. King
Murdoch University, Perth, WA, Australia
e-mail: Caroline.mansfield@murdoch.edu.au

L. King
e-mail: L.King@murdoch.edu.au

L. Papatraianou
Charles Darwin University, Adelaide, SA, Australia
e-mail: Lisa.Papatraianou@cdu.edu.au

S. McDonough
Federation University Australia, Mt. Helen, VIC, Australia
e-mail: s.mcdonough@federation.edu.au

Introduction

Over the last decade, initial teacher education (ITE) in Australia has undergone a plethora of changes in response to broader policy agendas aimed at improving the quality of graduates entering the teaching profession. Changes have entailed an explicit focus on the knowledge and skills developed in ITE through the implementation of Australian Professional Standards for Teaching (APST) (Australian Institute for Teaching and School Leadership (AITSL), 2011) and rigorous accreditation requirements for teacher education providers (AITSL, 2015a). Furthermore, the role of non-academic capabilities for teaching such as empathy, motivation and resilience has also come under scrutiny, and testing for these has become a suggested way of selecting teacher education candidates (AITSL, 2015b).

While understanding non-academic capabilities at the point of entry to teacher education has benefits and measuring such capabilities is indeed a strategy used in other professions, the extent to which some of the measured capabilities are innate and fixed, or alternatively can be developed over time and in a contextually responsive manner needs consideration. As Ungar argues, (2012) "to understand resilience we must explore the context in which the individual experiences adversity, making resilience first a quality of the broader social and physical ecology and second a quality of the individual" (p. 27). Uncertainty exists about the ways in which screening tests provide meaningful insight into the nature of resilience for pre-service teachers and of how teacher educators will embed opportunities in their programs for pre-service teachers to further enhance capacities that will enable them to deal with the complex and uncertain nature of teaching. As Connell (2009 p. 226) indicates, we cannot create a model of "the good teacher"; rather we need to employ the view of teachers that allows ITE to support diverse and creative approaches to teaching. A focus on the personal and contextual factors of resilience is central to this.

Alongside these developments, there has also been much research focused on teacher resilience. Gu (2014) argues that teacher resilience is both context and role specific and entails more than just "bouncing back". According to Gu and Day (2013), resilience for teachers is characterised by "the capacity to maintain equilibrium and a sense of commitment and agency in the everyday worlds in which teachers teach" (p. 26). Researchers in Australia have argued that teacher resilience is a capacity and process by which individuals draw on personal and contextual supports and engage effective strategies to manage challenges of the profession in a way that results in positive adaptation and professional growth (see, e.g., Strangeways & Papatraianou, 2017; Johnson et al., 2015). A focus on teacher resilience provides a way of supporting teachers to build personal resources for resilience (such as optimistic thinking, self-efficacy and problem-solving skills), understand how to mobilise contextual resources (such as seeking help from others) and build confidence for managing difficult situations.

With the current emphasis on teacher retention, teacher quality is an important element to take into account when examining teacher resilience. Motivation and commitment are central to teacher quality and enabling individuals to thrive makes for the "quality retention" of beginning teachers (Day & Gu, 2007, p. 1314). Research has shown that teacher effectiveness and commitment are related to teacher quality (Day & Gu, 2007) and are a key element to understanding the work, the lives and the effectiveness of teachers (Day, 2008). Day draws on the work of Crosswell's (2006) dimensions of commitment when describing his conception of resilience as "enduring commitment" (Day, 2008, p. 255). This enduring commitment is evident in passion; investment of "extra" time; a focus on the student; maintaining professional knowledge; transmitting knowledge and/or values; and engagement with the school community (Crosswell, 2006, pp. 111–112). In other words, sustaining these various dimensions of commitment means to "be resilient" (Day, 2008, p. 255) and it is not only about the physical retention of teachers, rather the quality of teachers remaining in the profession. However, it is also important to recognise that the stratification of the APST suggests a focus on improving the quality teachers. Yet the construction of the APST lends itself back to a focus on individual attributes of teachers. As argued by Connell (2009), "It embeds an individualized model of the teacher that is deeply problematic [... and ...] an arbitrary narrowing of practice" (p. 220). It is therefore pertinent to focus on teacher quality in a way that recognises the personal and contextual influences on teacher resilience and practice.

Within the context of ITE, few studies have investigated the resilience of pre-service teachers (see, e.g. Le Cornu, 2009). Yet it is well known that beginning teachers may experience "reality shock" (Friedman, 2004) or "praxis shock"; the umbrella terms used to describe the challenges experienced by beginning teachers, marking the transition from pre-service teacher to early career teacher. While this shock explains the increased rates of early career teacher attrition (Kelly, Reushle, Chakrabarty, & Kinnane, 2014), some authors blame insufficient preparation during ITE as the cause (Abbott-Chapman, 2005). Others report key contextual challenges such as physical and professional isolation, high workloads (Ballantyne, 2007), inadequate induction (Sharp, 2006) and "the condition of not knowing" can also contribute towards praxis shock (Corcoran, 1981, p. 20). For example, not knowing from whom to seek support and not knowing the norms, policies and procedures that operate within the school community can intensify feelings of praxis shock (Corcoran, 1981). Even so, how resilience may be developed in teacher education programs has been left largely to individual institutions and driven by teacher educator "champions". The importance of the explicit integration and teaching of resilience and well-being in ITE to combat such challenges is evident in new induction guidelines (AITSL, 2016) with professional identity and well-being comprising two of the four given areas for focus. However, the views of teacher educators in this field, to whom blame is often attributed, have been neglected. It is therefore timely for the voices of teacher educators to be heard and for the wealth of collective experience to inform policy and practice in ITE.

This chapter reports an empirical study of teacher educators' perceptions of teacher resilience and the role of teacher education programs in promoting resilience for pre-service teachers. Specifically, four research questions are explored:

1. How do teacher educators describe teacher resilience?
2. How do teacher educators perceive pre-service teachers to demonstrate their resilience?
3. What challenges do teacher educators describe pre-service teachers experiencing?
4. How do teacher educators perceive their role in promoting and facilitating resilience in teacher education?

Conceptual Framework

In this chapter, we conceptualise resilience from a social ecological perspective which emphasises the role of social and physical ecologies in the resilience process (Ungar, 2011). For pre-service teachers, such ecologies include the initial teacher education context (university- and faculty-/school-level influences such as degree structure, minors and specific units undertaken) and relationships with teacher educators. Sites of professional experience provide important "real-world" opportunities to build resilience through classroom teaching and relationships with students, colleagues, mentors and the broader school community. Influencing each of these levels is the broader "profession" including governmental and regulatory policies and practices (i.e. AITSL, teacher registration authorities, mandated curriculum and standardised testing) along with societal and community expectations of teachers. The process of building resilience for pre-service teachers involves the capacity to draw on personal and contextual resources to successfully navigate challenges at these multiple levels and to promote adaptive outcomes such as engagement, commitment and job fulfilment (Mansfield, Beltman, Weatherby-Fell, & Broadley, 2016).

Figure 6.1 illustrates the ecologies that may influence the resilience process for pre-service teachers. The vertical wedge represents the views of teacher educators on the contextual factors involved in the resilience process as per the aim of this study.

Methodology

Data were gathered from 73 Australian teacher educators as part of a larger study examining ways in which resilience can be embedded in higher education curriculum (Mansfield, 2016). An online survey consisting of open-ended questions was used to elicit their views regarding pre-service teacher resilience and the role of teacher educators and ITE courses in developing pre-service teacher resilience. Ethics approval for the study was granted by Murdoch University, and all participants were

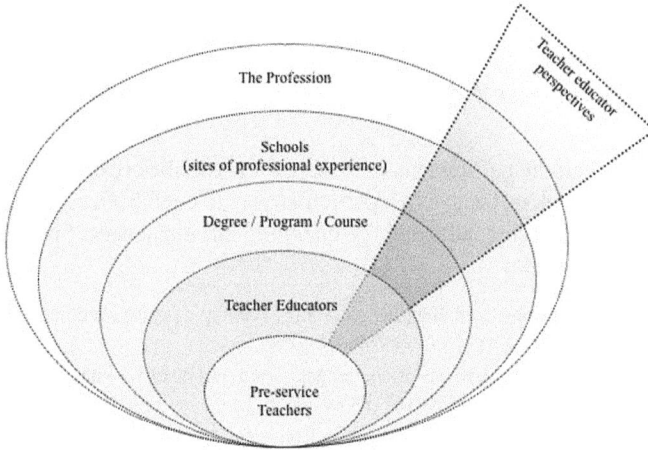

The Profession

Schools
(sites of professional experience)

Degree / Program / Course

Teacher Educators

Pre-service
Teachers

Teacher educator perspectives

Based on Bronfenbrenner,
1979; Cross & Hong, 2012.

Fig. 6.1 Teacher educator perspectives on ecologies that influence resilience for pre-service teachers

volunteers. All names and other specific identifiers have been changed to protect the participants' anonymity.

For each of the demographic questions, participants were given the option of "prefer not to say" and only 45% named their place of employment. Those named universities represented each state in Australia. Fifty-four participants gave their role, which included lecturers (28), senior lecturers (13), associate professors (5), program coordinators (5), one professor and one dean. Fifty-two taught in bachelor-level programs, 14 Graduate Diploma and 41 Master of Teaching. Thirty participants taught into Bachelor and Master of Teaching programs. Twenty-seven taught in early years' programs, 47 primary, 24 middle years and 43 secondary. Only 4 of the 73 participants had not previously been classroom teachers.

The data were analysed using thematic analysis (Braun & Clarke, 2006) and managed using NVivo 10. We first analysed the data by employing an inductive approach which enabled the identification of the common themes and patterns (Patton, 2002). We then analysed and re-coded these data independently to identify the key descriptive codes within these patterns. The data were then grouped and regrouped until we developed the conceptual framework for this study and the five key contexts relevant to the teacher educators' perspectives on pre-service teacher (PST) resilience. In the findings, the total number of participants identified within the broader conceptual framework is identified with n values. The thematic analysis is then reflective in the findings whereby the number of references from all participants is identified.

Findings

How Do Teacher Educators Describe Teacher Resilience?

More than half the participants (n = 48, 66%) described resilience as a "capacity" or "ability" to think or behave in a particular way to enable adaptive outcomes, despite challenges, obstacles, adversity or changing circumstances. Specific thoughts and behaviours include:

> managing emotions in challenging situations, keeping a positive attitude with students and not getting pulled down by circumstances (P8);
>
> ability to carry on regardless of challenges ... staying positive with students ... remaining cheerful, empathetic and focused (P45);
>
> being able to maintain your mental and physical "equilibrium" when the demands and expectations placed upon you keep you in a state of stress/anxiety (P9);
>
> sustain their work and their own well-being in the face of the many and often unexpected challenges that come with the role (P14);
>
> to step forward from setbacks ... learn from mistakes and search out solutions (P16); and
>
> reflect upon professional challenges ... by recognizing different and possible perspectives, and to respond to such challenges/setbacks with optimism, demonstrating a capacity to adapt, improve and change (P32).

Four respondents described resilience as a quality, personal attribute or characteristic, for example: *"a personal attribute that makes them suitable for the teaching profession"* (P69). Eleven respondents commented on the status of teacher resilience ranging from *"very poor"* (P22), *"fair—it could be better"* (P6) to *"bloody marvelous, considering what they have to do"* (P40).

How Do Teacher Educators Perceive Pre-service Teachers to Demonstrate Their Resilience?

Teacher educators observed pre-service teacher resilience in a range of ways. Most frequently noted was having a positive approach and optimistic outlook (26 references) through "willingness to learn" (P50) "having a go" (P67),"trying new ideas and being prepared to fail" (P44) and "participating actively in their learning" (P18). Overcoming challenges and recovering from setbacks (19 references) included "recovering from a poor grade" (P3), "facing challenges head-on" (P25) and "being 'real' about challenges and their outcomes" (P71). Perseverance and persistence were also noted (18 references) by "being willing to try something again" (P8), "keep on keeping on" (P17 and P34), "never giving up" (P17) and "continually striving to understand what makes a difference" (P4). Ways of responding to feedback also demonstrated resilience (15 references) "by choosing to respond positively to constructive feedback" (P2), by "accepting and acting on feedback, not taking criticisms personally" (P29) and by "asking for feedback on how they can improve, especially after a poor assessment result" (P51). Resilience was also seen through pre-service teachers' approaches to problem-solving (11 references) and capacity to cope (10 references) with stress, heavy workload and "demonstrating their ability to cope effectively in a wide variety of situations" (P19). The capacity to seek assistance when needed was noted (9 references) and building positive relationships (9 references), "developing professional relationships with tutors and other leaders and seeing the relevance of these relationships within and beyond the immediate environment" (P11). There were 8 references to flexibility and adaptability, including being "flexible and responsive" (P42) and "adapting to the constraints of situated practice" (P32).

What Challenges Do Teacher Educators Perceive Pre-service Teachers Experience?

Participants were asked for up to 10 responses to the question "What do you consider to be the main challenges pre-service teachers encounter when learning to become a teacher?" Responses indicated that pre-service teachers experienced personal challenges as well as challenges in school and university contexts.

Personal Challenges

Teacher educators noted that pre-service teachers often experience personal challenges during their teacher education experience (n = 69, 95%). These included 31 references to "juggling life/work/family/study commitments" (P2), time management (23 references), managing and "balancing workloads" (P22) (19 references), constructively responding to feedback (16 references), adopting a "teacher" mindset and developing "identity as teacher" (P39) (16 references), navigating conflicting beliefs between own experiences, university learning and schools (14 references), confidence (12 references), managing and being responsible for their own learning (12 references), professionalism and managing expectations (10 references each). Managing emotions, anxiety and mental health (8 references) was noted with the comment, "they need to be confident in the management of these issues before they can get in front of a class" (P30). Feeling overwhelmed and overloaded, along with financial challenges was also stated (8 references each).

Professional Experience Challenges

Similarly, challenges experienced in schools when on professional experience were noted. The most frequently mentioned was classroom, and more specifically, behaviour management (40 references) and "understanding how to respond to challenging students" (P2). "Navigating relationships with all stakeholders" (P28) could also be challenging (34 references). Colleagues could be "difficult or unsupportive" (P10), and pre-service teachers could have difficulty "understanding and reading what is appropriate interaction with colleagues" (P51) and "knowing how to deflect the negativity of older teaching staff" (P63). Similarly, parents may be "unsupportive of their child" (P51) or "question your practices" (P22). It could also be difficult to "support students who have troubled or traumatic home lives" (P29) and to "establish positive relationships with difficult students" (P36). Other challenges while in schools included planning and organisation (16 references) managing teaching, learning and assessment (24 references), lack of content knowledge (15 references) and meeting expectations (16 references). With regard to school culture, it was noted that some pre-service teachers experience difficulties "integrating into the school community" (P5), "understanding the system and the intricacies of school environments" (P42) and "dealing with the complex politics of a school staff" (P64) (18 references). Challenges with mentor relationships (12 references) were also mentioned—"unsupportive, even destructive, mentor teachers" (P62).

University Challenges

There were 95 references to the challenges pre-service teachers experience at university. Among these inadequate courses at university were most frequently mentioned (35 references) with specific examples of "crowded curriculum" (P10), lack of coherence through "disconnected assignments across units" (P9) and "too many assessments that are boring and not practical" (P21). Also noted were adjustment to university, lack of resources, online delivery and meeting course requirements.

How Do Teacher Educators Perceive Their Role in Promoting and Facilitating Resilience in Teacher Education and How Might This Be Enacted?

Role of Teacher Educators

In response to the question "What role do you think teacher educators play in helping pre-service teachers develop resilience?", 75% (n = 55) of participants provided insight into their roles with 25 references made to the important role teacher educators play in promoting and facilitating resilience. The "critical" (P60) role of teacher educators was reflected in responses such as "Teacher educators are essential in helping pre-service teachers develop resilience" (P35). Teacher educators identified a number of dimensions in their role in helping to develop resilience including: teaching skills and strategies that help foster resilience (25 references) such as "teach coping strategies, mindfulness, through problem-solving, use of case studies" (P36); providing support to pre-service teachers or to directing them to further avenues for support (23 references), and "supporting students to re-frame setbacks/failures as opportunities to improve and develop" (P41); modelling resilience (19 references) through their own practices, "I think teacher educators should model resiliency strategies" (P5); and the sharing of their own experiences and strategies (15 references), "As experienced teachers, it is incumbent upon them to share their tried and tested strategies and approaches with the pre-service teachers" (P45).

Other identified roles included teaching about the complexity and reality of life in schools (12 references) as a way of helping pre-service teachers to build resilience; "Discussions on the 'real life' of a teacher, time management, learning that failure is ok and can build resilience." (P44). Having "honest discussion" (P2) and conversations (11 references) were identified as part of the teacher educators' role as was their role in giving honest, constructive feedback and in prompting self-evaluation among pre-service teachers (7 references). Highlighting the importance of the concept of resilience for pre-service teachers was also regarded as part of a teacher educator's role (7 references), "it would help if all teacher educators could share and promote information about strategies for developing resilience" (P9).

Challenges in Promoting Resilience

While teacher educators indicated the central role they could hold in promoting and facilitating resilience, they also identified factors that make it challenging to enact, with one teacher educator commenting that "Teacher educators need to be everything to everyone!" (P23). There were 11 references to the way that the prior experiences of teacher educators might mediate their capacity to support the development of resilience, particularly if teacher educators had not previously held teaching positions in schools, "there are significant numbers of teacher educators who have not worked as teachers, or have little personal experience of the contemporary teaching environment" (P27). The workloads of academics and their responsibilities (8 references) were also seen as a potential barrier impacting on the ability of teacher educators to support the development of pre-service teachers' resilience, as it "requires a different mindset while trying to accommodate competing agendas" (P37). There were 5 references to an increasing "reliance on sessional staff who may not have support themselves or be aware of resources" (P26), as a context-specific challenge that may make it difficult to enact a focus on promoting resilience. Other challenges noted included the need for teacher educators themselves to have professional learning (5 references); deficit views of pre-service teachers (5 references); and teacher educators holding different views about whether building resilience was a valuable concept to focus on in initial teacher education (5 references).

More than half the respondents (n = 54, 74%) identified a range of challenges to embedding resilience in initial teacher education programs. The majority of the respondents identified that inadequacies in teacher education courses prevented such inclusions (35 references), explaining that programs were burdened with a crowded curriculum and time constraints (14 references); "it is such an overloaded course that you don't always get the opportunity to include these specific skills" given that "teacher education programs are highly regulated by multiple accrediting bodies" (P4). While individual teacher educators wanted to embed resilience in programs, "the major issue, just like in schools, is what gets taken out or how to fit it in" (P3) making it difficult to explicitly embed such skills within courses. Other program barriers included, to a lesser extent, conflicting views on what should be embedded across programs (6 references), a lack of coherence across programs (7 references) and a lack of resources (16 references) such as reduced funding and "time restraints prevent[ing] teacher educators from playing a bigger role in developing resilience." (P2) Other challenges included difficulties faced by pre-service teachers adjusting to university and program requirements (7 references), online delivery of courses and subsequently reduced opportunities to develop the necessary social skills that enable resilience (8 references).

Suggestions for Improvement

The majority of respondents (n = 68, 93%) identified ways in which embedding resilience in ITE programs could be improved. Embedding resilience specifically within professional experience components of programs was most commonly identified (48 references), with the need for these components to support connections between theory and practice (29 references); "there needs to be more continuity between university classes and school placements"(P1), and the importance of providing authentic learning contexts and awareness of realistic challenges of the profession; "explicit connection to real-world application of theory, supported and guide teaching practice opportunities, before and after going on practicum"(P5). Suitably appointed school-based mentors and university-based mentors (23 references) and partnerships between schools and universities were also identified as crucial to embedding resilience skills in professional experience programs to "enable greater in school connections between theory and practice where the tertiary staff, supervisors and leadership team meet with PSTs in a dialogical manner" (P60). However, 35 respondents advocated for the need to have a whole degree approach to designing curriculum and programs (51 references) "… although there is movement in this area, Australian HEPs [Higher Education Providers] tend to have a subject/unit/course focus rather than whole of program/degree focus as their organising framework for curriculum development. It takes a village to raise an ITE graduate" (P4). The need to explicitly teach skills within particular subjects across a program was also recognised (32 references). However, there was a lack of consensus as to how this could be accomplished.

Whether the respondents opted for a program approach or a specific focus of embedding resilience skills within professional experience courses, the importance of building better relationships between pre-service teachers, teacher educators and schools were identified as an important element to embedding resilience in courses and programs (37 references). Providing safe contexts in which pre-service teachers can discuss issues was central to these references; "a good network of support between the professional experience officers at the university and many of the site coordinators in school to ensure there is a consistency in understanding of students' responsibilities when at schools" (P2). A culture of "empowering and celebrating PSTs" (P9), offering "support and empathy to students" (P22), "a united value of [resilience] amongst faculty" (P28) and "valuing resilience as a vital non-academic attribute for teachers to have/develop" (P1) were identified as important facets of developing such relationships within programs.

Discussion

The findings of this study highlight the critical role that teacher education plays in the development of resilience for pre-service teachers and provide insight into the ways that a focus on pre-service teacher resilience could be developed further within teacher education programs. Concerning our conceptual framework, the multiple layers of context at the personal (pre-service teacher), program and university (teacher educators), school (practising teachers) and profession (regulatory, societal) levels are potential spaces for the development of teacher resilience. Along with personal development opportunities, which may also be age appropriate for pre-service teachers entering teacher education directly from secondary school, teacher education experiences at university and in a variety of school settings enable a range of resilience-related strategies and skills to be developed in multiple authentic contexts. For example, learning to respond to feedback in a professional manner, developing realistic expectations, learning to work with mentors and negotiate collegial relationships, managing the roller coaster of emotions and learning strategies for self-preservation. In the development of teacher resilience, both context and role are critical (Gu, 2014).

Perhaps not surprisingly, the majority of respondents were in support of the idea of embedding resilience more explicitly in teacher education curriculum. Even so, structural barriers such as crowded curriculum and time constraints, policy and regulatory processes and the need for stronger partnerships between schools and universities were cited. Other barriers such as valuing and adequately resourcing resilience in the curriculum and overcoming entrenched practices and perspectives suggest that there may also be the need for a cultural shift in teacher education practices. With respect to supporting pre-service teacher resilience, respondents mentioned relational strategies, such as providing a high level of pastoral care, strengthening partnerships with stakeholders and providing realistic expectations and experiences. Teacher educators themselves were also seen to provide support through keeping up to date with current practice and their own role modelling of resilience in their daily work. These findings speak to the structural, curricular and policy challenges while at the same time highlighting the critical relational and personal supports for resilience in teacher education. The data show the importance of considering the issue on a range of levels and in a range of contexts, as illustrated in Fig. 6.1.

A thought-provoking finding is the view articulated by some respondents that teacher education curriculum in their institutions lacks coherence and relevance and that teacher educators themselves hinder through engaging in practices that do not explicitly model, embed or allow for discussion of the way resilience enables pre-service teachers to navigate the complexity and uncertainty of teaching. The issue of coherence "based on a common, clear vision of good teaching grounded in an understanding of learning" has been identified as a best practice principle for teacher education programs (Darling-Hammond, 2005a, cited in Ingvarson et al., 2014, p. x). However, the views of some respondents from this study echo an earlier statement that, "creating coherence has been difficult in teacher education because of departmental divides, individualistic norms, and the hiring of part-time adjunct instructors in some institutions that have used teacher education as a "cash cow" rather than an investment in our nation's future" (Darling-Hammond, 2006, p. 306).

The emphasis on the role of context in these findings raises questions about the issue of testing for "resilience" as a screening measure to be considered in a different light. If the degree to which an individual demonstrates resilience is also dependent on the context, perceived relational support and explicit teaching of skills and strategies that support the resilience process, then a "pretest" for teacher resilience may not provide an accurate assessment of resilience in an authentic context. While it may be useful to identify general outlook and attitudes, or the way in which resilience is demonstrated in their lives prior to teaching, the extent to which this predicts career resilience has not been verified. We argue that resilience develops with experience, within context, and over time and therefore, needs to be explicitly modelled, taught and embedded in teacher education curriculum.

Implications

This study has a number of implications for teacher education and the work of teacher educators. With respect to teacher education curriculum, there seems an enthusiasm for clearer and more explicit direction for ways to support and enhance pre-service teacher resilience. Teacher educators themselves, however, may need professional learning about non-cognitive capacities of teachers, including resilience. Many teacher educators rely almost exclusively on their own school teaching experience to inform their pedagogy in teacher education and as argued by Goodwin and Kosnick (2013), "teacher educators need formal preparation and induction" (p. 343). Similarly, Loughran (2014) contends that "professional development of teacher educators must be purposefully conceptualized, thoughtfully implemented, and meaningfully employed" (p. 280). We argue that teacher educators require opportunities to engage in collective, shared professional learning about the resilience process and contextual approaches within teacher education programs that foster and support the development of pre-service teacher resilience.

In times of uncertainty and complexity, where context matters, the development of resilience among pre-service teachers is especially critical, not only for survival but for sustained effectiveness and growth. Loughran and Hamilton (2016) argue that "learning to teach is far more about an educative experience rather than an approach to training" (p. 4), contending that pre-service teachers need to be able to deal with the complex, dynamic and uncertain nature of teaching. Along with the development of pedagogical skills and content knowledge, we argue that to navigate the uncertain and complex world of teaching, pre-service teachers require the opportunity and time to develop strategies and skills that support resilience in multiple and authentic contexts throughout their initial teacher education programs. Assessing teacher resilience as an innate, predetermined capacity that pre-service teachers may or may not possess is contrary to much of the recent research in the field.

Embedding contextually based approaches to the development of pre-service teacher resilience in teacher education programs requires further consideration of how resilience is viewed in policy and by the profession. There is a silence in the Australian Professional Standards for Teachers about teacher well-being and resilience, and as noted earlier in this chapter, while teacher well-being and resilience are included in AITSL (2016) induction guidelines, these are not explicitly acknowledged in the Standards. In the same way that personal and social capabilities are important in The Australian Curriculum for schools and "in developing and acting with personal and social capability, students become confident, resilient and adaptable" (ACARA, 2012) we argue that similar capabilities should be explicit in the Australian Professional Standards for Teachers.

The issue of program coherence identified in the findings of this research also has broader implications for the nature of policy in teacher education and where a focus on supporting the development of pre-service teacher resilience sits in relation to current policy directions. Policy agendas which regard teacher education as being able to "train students of teaching so that they are 'classroom ready'" (Loughran & Hamilton, 2016, p. 4) neglect the complex relationships that exist in teaching and learning. Moving beyond a technical, what works approach to teacher education towards one which recognises that the "teaching and learning of teaching matters" (Loughran, 2016, p. 258), requires a shift in policy agendas. Such a shift requires attention to both the unique pedagogy of teacher education; the role, practice and professional development of teacher educators themselves; and a recognition in policy and in the APST of the ways that non-cognitive attributes, such as resilience, are developmental and grounded in context.

This study has provided insight into a previously neglected area of research about the ways teacher educators perceive pre-service teacher resilience. Crowe and Berry (2007) argue that research enables teacher educator practice to be made "explicit, not only to themselves, but also more broadly to the community of teacher educators" (p. 31), and while the findings of the research indicate the key role that teacher educators can play in modelling, teaching and supporting the development of pre-service teacher resilience, future research is needed that explores the ways teacher educators are embedding approaches to resilience within teacher education programs.

Initial work in mapping the ways teacher educators are embedding contextually based approaches to resilience has occurred through a National Teaching Fellowship (Mansfield, 2016)—"Staying BRiTE: Promoting resilience in higher education" (www.stayingbrite.edu.au). This ongoing work has involved collaboration with colleagues at 6 Australian universities and key stakeholders (partner schools, Departments of Education, AITSL) to embed resilience in teacher education programs in ways that are contextually responsive and take into account location, demographics and student needs. Authentic cases illustrating approaches to building resilience have been developed (see www.stayingbrite.edu.au/authentic cases) as well as resources to assist teacher educators.

These authentic cases serve as exemplars of how teacher educators can embed the explicit teaching of resilience within their everyday work, in ways that are relevant to their context and in ways that address some of the concerns of teacher educators identified in this paper. The authentic cases serve as a reminder that individual championing can lead to meaningful changes within ITE. As argued earlier, providing the opportunity for teacher educators to respond to issues of inadequate ITE preparation and early career teacher attrition, for which they are often blamed, has given them a voice to articulate the many contexts and stakeholders responsible for PST resilience. These changes can have a significant impact on PST resilience in ways that not only addresses some of the concerns identified by teacher educators in this paper but recognises the importance of advocating for the integration of resilience in ITE in ways that prepare graduates for a profession that not only requires resilience but demands it.

References

Abbott-Chapman, J. (2005). Let's keep our beginning teachers! *Principal Matters: The Official Journal of the Secondary Principals' Associations of Australia, Summer*, 2–4.

Australian Curriculum Assessment and Reporting Authority. (2012). *Australian Curriculum*. Retrieved from http://www.australiancurriculum.edu.au/.

Australian Institute for Teaching and School Leadership (AITSL). (2011). *Australian national professional standards for teachers*. Victoria: Education Services Australia.

Australian Institute for Teaching and School Leadership (AITSL). (2015a). *Accreditation of initial teacher education programs in Australia: Standards and procedures*. Melbourne: AITSL.

Australian Institute for Teaching and School Leadership (AITSL). (2015b). *Action now: Selection of entrants into initial teacher education*. Melbourne: AITSL. Retrieved from http://www.aitsl.edu.au/initial-teacher-education/ite-reform/selection.

Australian Institute for Teaching and School Leadership (AITSL). (2016). *Graduate to proficient: Australian guidelines for teacher induction into the profession* (978-1925192-40-7). Victoria, Australia: Australian Institute for Teaching and School Leadership. Retrieved from http://aitsl.edu.au/induction/guidelines.

Ballantyne, J. (2007). Documenting praxis shock in early-career Australian music teachers: The impact of pre-service teacher education. *International Journal of Music Education, 25*(3), 181–191.

Braun, V., & Clarke, V. (2006). Using thematic analysis in psychology. *Qualitative Research in Psychology, 3*(2), 77–101.

Connell, R. (2009). Good teachers on dangerous ground: Towards a new view of teacher quality and professionalism. *Critical Studies in Education, 50*(3), 213–229.

Corcoran, E. (1981). Transition shock: The beginning teacher's paradox. *Journal of Teacher Education, 32*(3), 19–23.

Crosswell, L. (2006). *Understanding teacher commitment in times of change* (Unpublished doctoral dissertation). Queensland University of Technology, Queensland, Australia.

Crowe, A. R., & Berry, A. (2007). Teaching prospective teachers to think like a teacher: Articulating our principles of practice. In T. Russell & J. Loughran (Eds.), *Enacting a pedagogy of teacher education* (pp. 31–44). London: Routledge.

Darling-Hammond, L. (2006). Constructing 21st-century teacher education. *Journal of Teacher Education, 57*(3), 300–314. https://doi.org/10.1177/0022487105285962.

Day, C. (2008). Committed for life? Variations in teachers' work, lives and effectiveness. *Journal of Educational Change, 9*(3), 243–260.

Day, C., & Gu, Q. (2007). Variations in the conditions for teachers' professional learning and development: Sustaining commitment and effectiveness over a career. *Oxford Review of Education, 33*(4), 423–443.

Friedman, I. A. (2004). Directions in teacher training for low-burnout teaching. In E. Frydenberg (Ed.), *Thriving, surviving, or going under: Coping with everyday lives* (pp. 305–326). Greenwich, CT: Information Age Publishing.

Goodwin, A. L., & Kosnik, C. (2013). Quality teacher educators = quality teachers? Conceptualizing essential domains of knowledge for those who teach teachers. *Teacher Development, 17*(3), 334–346. https://doi.org/10.1080/13664530.2013.813766.

Gu, Q. (2014). The role of relational resilience in teachers' career-long commitment and effectiveness. *Teachers and Teaching: Theory and Practice, 20*(5), 502–529. https://doi.org/10.1080/13540602.2014.937961.

Gu, Q., & Day, C. (2013). Challenges to teacher resilience: Conditions count. *British Educational Research Journal, 39*(1), 22–44. https://doi.org/10.1080/01411926.2011.623152.

Ingvarson, L., Reid, K., Buckley, S., Kleinhenz, E., Masters, G., & Rowley, G. (2014). *Best practice teacher education programs and Australia's own programs.* Canberra: Australian Council for Educational Research.

Johnson, J., Down, B., Le Cornu, R., Peters, J., Sullivan, A., Pearce, J., et al. (2015). *Early career teachers: Stories of resilience.* London: Springer.

Kelly, N., Reushle, S., Chakrabarty, S., & Kinnane, A. (2014). Beginning teacher support in Australia: Towards an online community to augment current support. *Australian Journal of Teacher Education, 39*(4), 68–82. https://doi.org/10.14221/ajte.2014v39n4.6.

Le Cornu, R. (2009). Building resilience in pre-service teachers. *Teaching and Teacher Education, 25*(5), 717–723. https://doi.org/10.1016/j.tate.2008.11.016.

Loughran, J. (2014). Professionally developing as a teacher educator. *Journal of Teacher Education, 65*(4), 271–283. https://doi.org/10.1177/0022487114533386.

Loughran, J. (2016). Teaching and teacher education: The need to go beyond rhetoric. In R. Brandenberg, S. McDonough, J. Burke, & S. White (Eds.), *Teacher education: Innovation, intervention and impact* (pp. 253–264). Singapore: Springer.

Loughran, J., & Hamilton, M. L. (2016). Developing an understanding of teacher education. In J. Loughran & M. L. Hamilton (Eds.), *International handbook of teacher education* (pp. 3–22). https://doi.org/10.1007/978-981-10-0366-0_1.

Mansfield, C. F. (2016). *Promoting resilience in higher education: A collaborative approach to curriculum development for student resilience in teacher education.* Office of Learning and Teaching, National Teaching Fellowship.

Mansfield, C. F., Beltman, S., Weatherby-Fell, N., & Broadley, T. (2016). Classroom ready? Building resilience in teacher education. In R. Brandenberg, S. McDonough, J. Burke, & S. White (Eds.), *Teacher education: Innovation, intervention and impact* (pp. 211–229). Singapore: Springer.

Patton, M. Q. (2002). *Qualitative research and evaluation methods* (3rd ed.). Thousand Oaks, CA: Sage Publications.

Sharp, H. (2006). *Examining the consequences of inadequate induction for beginning teachers*. Refereed Paper Presented at the Annual Conference of the Australian Association for Research in Education, Adelaide.

Strangeways, A., & Papatraianou, L. H. (2017). Remapping the landscape of resilience: Learning from an Arrernte teacher's story. In *Knowledge Intersections: Exploring the Research of Central Australia Symposium*, Alice Springs.

Ungar, M. (2011). The social ecology of resilience: Addressing contextual and cultural ambiguity of a nascent construct. *American Journal of Orthopsychiatry, 81*(1), 1–17. https://doi.org/10.1111/j.1939-0025.2010.01067.x.

Author Biographies

Caroline Mansfield is an Associate Professor and Associate Dean of Research in the School of Education, Murdoch University, Western Australia. Her research focuses on teachers and students with an emphasis on motivation, well-being and resilience. She has lead two large projects about teacher resilience—Keeping Cool and BRiTE. In 2016, she was awarded a National Teaching Fellowship (Staying BRiTE: Promoting resilience in higher education) to lead a team of colleagues across Australia to embed resilience in teacher education programs (www.stayingbrite.edu.au) and build a national and international network of interested researchers and practitioners. Her future research will continue to explore innovative approaches to promote resilience in education and how school communities can support resilience.

Lisa Papatraianou is Senior Lecturer in Education—Professional Learning in the School of Education at Charles Darwin University. She has expertise in the conceptual and theoretical contributions to the field of human resilience and the practical application of resilience in education, psychology, social work and social policy. Her research focuses on resilience across the lifespan and in a variety of educational contexts with her current research focusing on the resilience of teachers, teacher educators and young people. In 2017, she was awarded the Australian Teacher Education Association's (ATEA) University-School Partnership Award and grant focused on understanding diverse students' resilience. She is a Maurice de Rohan Scholar and was an Australian Endeavour Post-doctoral Research Fellow at Goldsmiths College, University of London.

Sharon McDonough is Senior Lecturer in the Faculty of Education and Arts at Federation University Australia. Her research focuses on self-study of teacher educator practices, teacher emotion and embodiment and mentoring. In 2013, she was awarded an Office of Learning and Teaching National Citation for Outstanding Contributions to Student Learning, and since 2015, she has been a member of the Australian Teacher Education Association (ATEA) where she holds the HDR/ECR portfolio. She is also interested in the role social media plays in academic work and is the Australian host of Shut Up and Write Tuesdays, a virtual writing workshop for academics. She writes a regular column, Text, Twitter and Tweet for Practical Literacy, a publication of the Australian Literacy Educators' Association, which focuses on the use of social media and digital technologies in teaching.

Laura King is a research assistant and project manager across various projects in several Schools, including the School of Education at Murdoch University in Western Australia. She previously worked for a decade as a chartered professional engineer/project manager for government, academia, industry and consultancy. She also holds a Ph.D. in professional writing, editing and publishing and is a sessional academic in professional and creative writing, and communication skills. She has been a finalist for the Western Australian Young Achiever (Career) award.

Chapter 7
Self-regulatory Practices: Key Aspects of Learning for Student Teachers on Practicum

Lyn McDonald

Abstract The role the visiting lecturer plays in promoting and supporting student teacher learning on practicum is an important one in Initial Teacher Education (ITE). A central argument of this chapter is that student teacher learning is not simply focussed on surviving the practicum and meeting set requirements, but in being challenged to acquire the skills and practices of self-regulated learning and the development of adaptive expertise, an integral part of being an effective teacher. Interpretive, qualitative methodology was used to investigate the role three visiting lecturers played in the development of these skills. One of the pivotal findings emphasised the importance of the conversations that took place between the visiting lecturer, associate teacher and student teacher promoting self-regulatory practices. The incorporation of these self-regulatory skills by visiting lecturers and associate teachers, supporting student teachers and their learning should be a central part of any professional development programmes.

Keywords Self-regulation · Practicum · Visiting lecturer · Pre-service teacher
Adaptive expertise · Triadic/professional discussions · Associate teacher

Introduction

The practicum or professional experience can be a complex, challenging and high-stakes environment for pre-service teachers. One of the reasons it is a high-stakes situation is because of the tension around assessment, and the passing or failing of the practicum. Therefore, as student teachers (pre-service teachers) make sense of their own capabilities, and develop confidence and identity as teachers (Koerner, Rust, & Baumgartner, 2002), it is important for them to develop self-regulatory

L. McDonald (✉)
University of Auckland, Auckland, New Zealand
e-mail: l.mcdonald@auckland.ac.nz

© Springer Nature Singapore Pte Ltd. 2018   99
D. Heck and A. Ambrosetti (eds.), *Teacher Education In and For Uncertain Times*,
https://doi.org/10.1007/978-981-10-8648-9_7

skills and practices in order to optimise their learning and teaching progress. This chapter aims to discuss the effective practices of three visiting lecturers (university teacher educators) supported by associate teachers (mentor teachers) working together, engaging student teachers in critically reflective discussions in support of self-regulatory practices.

The construct of self-regulation in learning was developed from the assumption that learners "exercise agency by consciously controlling and intervening in their learning" (Winne & Hadwin, 2008, p. 297). There are a range of definitions that describe the process of self-regulation. Zimmerman (2008), a seminal writer in the field, described self-regulation as learning that is guided by metacognition, goal setting, cognitive engagement or changes in motivation. Perry, Hutchinson and Thauberger (2008) described self-regulated learners as those who "exercise metacognition by analysing the demands of tasks in relation to their strengths and weaknesses as learners ... and are motivated to learn" (p. 97). Further, Perry et al. (2008) described student teachers who exhibited self-regulation, as those who believed in the chance to take on challenging tasks in order to extend their own learning. It could therefore be argued, developing the skills and strategies of self-regulation support and promote student teachers in their goal of becoming flexible and adaptive in their learning and teaching progress (Donovan, Bransford & Pellegrino, 2008).

Social psychologists (e.g., Zimmerman, 2000) view self-regulated learning in terms of three phases. The first phase, forethought and planning, is one which self-regulated learners engage in prior to learning and the planning of goals is an integral component of the forethought phase within the context of learning to teach. It is important for student teachers in this first phase to plan challenging and relevant learning goals, with support and encouragement from visiting lecturers and associate teachers. It is through these processes of self-regulation that student teachers refer to their own cognitive processes (knowledge), and the subsequent monitoring of the associated processes (skilfulness) and, in the development of such skilfulness, a sense of self-regulation (Hattie, 2009).

It is during the second phase, the performance monitoring phase, in which learners engage in metacognitive, cognitive and motivational processes including the key features of self-observation and self-control (Zimmerman, 2002, 2008). Self-observation involves the use of metacognitive strategies that assist learners in evaluating their performance (Zimmerman, 2008). Self-control strategies assist student teachers in managing the task they have set themselves, to enhance motivation and focus attention. Further, when learners combine these two features of self-observation and self-control by engaging in the task, they are motivated to continue working to attain their goals (Zimmerman, 2008).

An important part of the performance monitoring phase is the feedback learners receive from others because through feedback learners can gauge their progress and commitment to the goal which they have set (Locke & Latham, 2002). It is in the constructing of feedback that the visiting lecturer and associate teacher play an important role, by guiding and supporting student teachers in the setting, monitoring, and evaluation of goals and giving feedback and feed-forward on their progress. Visiting lecturers should encourage student teachers to ask the questions "Where am I going? (What are the goals?) How am I going? (What progress is being made towards the goal?) Where to next? (What activities need to be undertaken to make better progress?) consistent with the notions of feedback and feed-forward" (Hattie & Timperley, 2007, p. 86).

The third and final phase of self-regulation is evaluation and reflection on performance. It is in this phase that learners evaluate their performance with reference to the learning goals set, the effectiveness of learning strategies used and their management of motivation and engagement (Zimmerman, 2000, 2002). The processes of evaluation and reflection during practicum are important aspects of all triadic/professional discussions (three-way conversations) for visiting lecturers, associate teachers and student teachers. One of the aims of these discussions is to provide formative feedback to the student teachers on their teaching and learning progress, set future goals and engage the student teachers in reflective conversation. The other purpose is to complete a summative assessment. Throughout all three phases of self-regulation, it is important that learners have a belief in their own ability to achieve their tasks and learning goals, because the perceptions and beliefs learners hold about their learning and goal achievement, underpins self-regulation (Zimmerman, 2000, 2002).

There are many benefits of learning the skills and practices of self-regulation for student teachers in ITE. By teaching student teachers to be more self-regulatory, they may experience greater success in being motivated to achieve, develop lifelong learning skills and strategies, and, as a consequence, prepare them for the setting of more challenging goals and learning tasks (Zimmerman, 2002).

Researchers (e.g., Buzza, Kotsopoulos, Mueller & Johnston, 2013) commented that "literature on teacher learning has shown links between being a self-regulated learner, reflecting effectively on one's own practice and being an adaptive expert" (p. 1). Further, adaptive expertise requires the acquisition of several cognitive, affective and motivational components (de Corte, 2010). These components, so important in student teacher learning include: a well organised and flexibly accessible domain-specific knowledge base; heuristic methods; meta-knowledge; self-regulatory skills and positive beliefs about oneself as a learner (de Corte, 2010, p. 46). Therefore, to be an adaptive expert, a student teacher needs to be a self-regulated learner which "... involves the willingness and ability to change core competencies" and to continually strive to develop one's expertise (Bransford, Derry, Berliner, Hammerness, & Beckett, 2005, p. 223).

In the current chapter, the theoretical lens brought to studying the partnerships between schools and universities is one focused on the relationship between the visiting lecturer, associate teacher and student teacher. The visiting lecturer in the Faculty of Education (where the larger research study was based) has an important role and responsibility in the monitoring, guidance and assessment of student teachers' professional growth, and is required to be a registered teacher who is knowledgeable and experienced in ITE. The role of the associate teacher is to monitor, guide and mentor student teachers, assess the student teacher's professional growth in collaboration with the visiting lecturer, and act as the conduit person between the student teacher and the teaching profession.

The professional supervision of student teachers is seen as a collaborative process and liaison between the visiting lecturer and associate teacher. It is the nature of the partnership that is crucial, one focused on both partners working together, utilising the knowledge, skills and expertise of both, by empowering the student teacher to self-regulate their own learning through goal setting, reflection and effective pedagogy. The partnership recognising and respecting the different, but equally important roles both visiting lecturer and associate teacher play in supporting student teacher learning, requires a high-trust approach. Trust in a complementary partnership involves "specific expectations of role relationships and is seen as a vital ingredient in the work of schools" (Tschannen-Moran, 2001, p. 57).

Method

Interpretive, qualitative methodology was used to investigate the role the visiting lecturer played in student teacher learning. Seven visiting lecturers (VL), 18 student teachers (ST) and 18 associate teachers (AT) participated in a larger research study from two different teacher education programmes at a Faculty of Education. In this chapter, data from semi-structured interviews, focus group interviews, initial practicum meetings, triadic/professional discussions and documentation are reported.

The sampling method was both purposive for the programmes, practicums, schools, student teachers, and associate teachers and convenience sampling for the visiting lecturers as the researcher had potential access to them through employment at the university. Once the visiting lecturers had volunteered to participate in the research study, purposive sampling was utilised in the selection of the student teachers. A request for schools to participate was sent out, and the 18 associate teachers who were supervising the 18 student teachers on practicum were invited to participate in the larger research study. None of the associate teachers and student teachers were known to the researcher.

Data analysis was completed using a thematic approach. Thematic analysis seeks to identify concepts and themes that can be deduced and/or induced from the data: "… while the general issues that are of interest are determined prior to analysis, the specific nature of the categories and themes to be explored are not pre-determined" (Ezzy, 2002, p. 88). Using an inductive approach meant the themes identified during the coding process in the study were strongly linked to the emerging data or data themselves. Some of the themes that emerged in the larger research study were, for example, complementary partnerships, self-regulation of learning and feedback/feed-forward.

Open coding took a number of forms, and the researcher was looking for anything 'new' that would push the boundaries of the research and link to the research question(s). Axial coding was the second stage of coding used in the research study, namely to look for relationships between and among themes that emerged from the open coding. Selective coding was the third stage used to guide and inform the 'story' being told. The deductive approach to the analysis utilised the themes based on the researcher's own theoretical knowledge of, for example, student teacher learning on practicum.

Ethical issues included in this chapter are voluntary participation, informed consent and the protection of confidentiality and anonymity. Voluntary participation and informed consent were gained from the Dean of the Faculty of Education, Principals of Schools, visiting lecturers, associate teachers and student teachers. It was therefore important that the Dean, School Principals and all other participants were assured that involvement in the larger research study would be kept private and confidential. Pseudonyms were used in the coding and reporting of the data, and participants were assured that the use of pseudonyms would also apply to any resultant academic dissemination.

Theoretical Framework

Learning to teach is both complex and demanding, and support for student teachers from the visiting lecturer and associate teacher can be crucial in this process. To effectively regulate learning, there is a necessity for student teachers to acquire a professional knowledge base, that is, a blend of content, curriculum and pedagogical knowledge which is necessary to teach children (Darling-Hammond & Bransford, 2005). This chapter investigates the role three visiting lecturers played in promoting and supporting student teacher learning, working in a complementary partnership with associate teachers. It will be argued in this chapter that key learning, such as the development of self-regulatory skills, are important strategies for student teachers to acquire for the promotion of their learning and development towards becoming a teacher.

As described in the previous section, there are three distinct phases of self-regulation described by Zimmerman (2000). In this chapter, the forethought and planning phase involved student teachers on practicum analysing the necessary learning tasks, and setting goals towards their completion with support from visiting lecturers and associate teachers. The performance monitoring phase comprised student teachers employing strategies to make progress on their learning tasks and goals, self-monitoring the effectiveness of those strategies and recognising the required motivation for completion of the tasks. Furthermore, in this phase, was the ability by student teachers to implement feedback from visiting lecturers and associate teachers. In the third phase, the evaluation of performance phase, student teachers evaluated and reflected on the success or otherwise of their performance of the set learning tasks and goals and their selected strategy for achievement of the tasks and goals. This phase occurred during the triadic/professional discussions. This chapter is framed around one key question: What are the key self-regulatory practices used by three visiting lecturers in supporting student teacher learning on practicum?

Findings

A key finding was that three visiting lecturers (VLs 1, 2 and 3) were highly effective at promoting student teachers' self-regulatory skills and practices. They were effective because they challenged and questioned learning, encouraged reflection and risk-taking, provided feedback and feed-forward, and promoted relevant goal setting. It was also apparent during the triadic/professional discussions that these visiting lecturers supported the student teachers in connecting their teaching and learning progress to their knowledge of learners, learning, content and pedagogical content knowledge. There are four themes reported in this section (through the three phases of self-regulation): goal setting, risk-taking, acting on feedback and partnerships with associate teachers.

The following description by VL2 in her interview was typical of the three visiting lecturers in the initial stage of their work with their student teachers, conveying the importance of self-regulation and goal setting to learning, and the identification of strategies and resources to achieve the set goals:

> Student teachers need to understand the importance of setting goals around some aspect of learning they need to become more informed about. So I get them to goal set, to identify strategies, or what resources or what skills they need to actually utilize. They should be building and understanding some aspect of their practice they don't have a good understanding of when setting goals.

She continued by saying that, when she talked to the student teachers about goal setting at the initial practicum meeting, she asked them what their particular goal meant for their personal learning. VL2 questioned ST2 in an email communication, "Where can you go to find out more information about your own goal, who can you talk to? Why that goal? What will you focus on?"

VL1 also asked student teachers at the initial practicum meeting to consider whether their particular goals were challenging enough, and to draw on prior experiences and areas of strength and weakness:

> What are your personal goals for this practicum? What is it you want to achieve? What do you want to come out of this practicum? What will challenge you? Think about last practicum and where you want to improve your teaching and learning? Your goals need to be challenging and relevant to you.

ST13 elaborated:

> We have just been learning about differentiated teaching and learning at university—in theory it all sounds wonderful but I want to learn how to put all that knowledge into practice.

VL1 talked to the student teachers at the initial meeting in the first week of practicum of her expectation that they become self-regulating and reflective in their learning. VL1 also commented that, with the acceptance of responsibility for their own learning, student teachers would need to be aware of enhanced risk-taking. She said to the student teachers that risk-taking and innovation in teaching was about moving into areas of teaching they had not ventured into before.

She spoke to the student teachers about being able to:

… reflect on your own practice and pedagogy. Look at yourselves and think what I can do that is going to make a difference in this particular learning situation. If things go wrong you can see what you need to do to adapt a lesson or to adapt some ideas to make those changes.

VL1 reported in her interview that she encouraged the student teachers to take risks in goal setting. She stated, "I believe that risk is an important part of student teachers' teaching and learning. If they only ever do things safely then they're never going to learn anything and never actually make any difference in their teaching".

VL3 in her interview emphasised she encouraged the student teachers to be proactive about their practice of monitoring their goals in the second phase of self-regulation and stated:

Our conversations are always about unpacking where the student teachers think they are at, what they think they are doing well and where they think they need to work. So where they are at … and getting them to talk through where they feel they have improved or what are the things they are focusing on, to develop or to modify.

The 10 student teachers monitored and evaluated their own learning progress in relation to their goals and were encouraged in the process by VLs 1, 2 and 3. Three student teachers stated in the focus group interviews that they audio-recorded or video-recorded a number of lessons (with the focus being on their goal) over the five weeks, watched the lesson and evaluated their progress towards achieving the goals. An example was ST12 who commented, "I found that so useful for my own learning and for areas still to be worked on". ST12 also made the point, "[t]o assist with the monitoring of my own goals I asked the children in the class for feedback and then changed teaching practices accordingly". Similarly ST1 stated, "I used the feedback from my visiting lecturer (VL1) and my associate teacher to make changes and evaluate where I was in relation to my goal".

The three visiting lecturers and associate teachers gave student teachers constructive, regular feedback on their goals throughout the practicum. The feedback was sometimes verbal given at the initial meetings, informal meetings and tri-adic/professional discussions but also consisted of written feedback. Further, the feedback related to the development of self-regulatory strategies rather than focussed on the task or the self. VL3 asked the student teachers to keep going back to their goals and monitor their own progress. She commented in her interview:

Feedback on the goals should lead to student teachers self-regulating their own learning and monitoring their own progress. It's asking them to think about their goals and considering—how am I going with that, what were my successes, what were my challenges, I need to do more of this.

At the triadic/professional discussion, VL1 asked for AT2's feedback on ST13's progress in her practicum, and what particular learning goals ST13 could focus on in the future:

VL1: What would you suggest are the things that [ST13] still needs to work on?

AT2: Planning probably. There's been a lot of changing over the last couple of years in the way that we plan and that's directly resulting from the kind of shift in pedagogy to negotiated learning …

Similarly, VL3 described how she encouraged an evaluation by the student teachers (with the associate teachers) on the achievement of their goals, thus identifying strengths and weaknesses:

> I'm really looking for a student teacher's ability to critically reflect on their teaching and rather than just saying it went 'well, the children liked it and I'm saying well I'm really pleased they liked it.' That was nice but did they learn anything and how do you know they've learnt and what evidence have you got to show that they've achieved the learning outcomes that you have for them?

Discussion

The findings reported in the previous section indicated that if there are skilled visiting lecturers and associate teachers using high-quality practices of collaboration, challenge and support, they are able to encourage student teachers to develop the skills and strategies of self-regulated learning, and thus develop a foundation to becoming adaptive experts. These practices included student teachers being encouraged to critically reflect on their learning on practicum, evaluating the effectiveness of teaching strategies utilised, and having taken risks in their teaching being prepared to discuss the outcomes.

Williams (2014) commented on the importance of teachers and academics working together with the possibility of rich professional learning for all. One key finding in this chapter emphasised the importance of the conversations that took place between the visiting lecturer, associate teacher and student teacher highlighting self-regulatory practices. The effective visiting lecturers recognised the knowledge and contributions of associate teachers in the conversations in support of student teachers and their learning. Each of the two parties has a unique role to play, and both visiting lecturers and associate teachers should recognise what each party contributes to ITE and learn from each other (Timperley, 2001).

In the first phase, the forethought and planning phase, the effective visiting lecturers (with associate teachers) assisted student teachers by helping them identify challenging and appropriate learning goals, and strategically planned learning opportunities to focus on. It was important in this phase that student teachers saw the value of their set goals to their personal learning, and the support of visiting lecturers and associate teachers was crucial. Without explicit learning goals, it is difficult to know what counts as evidence of students' learning so the setting of clear, explicit learning goals is essential (Hiebert, Morris, Berk & Jansen, 2007). Further, student teachers at this stage of their learning needed to believe they were able to attain the set learning goal (efficacy expectation) and feel they were able to achieve the goal through the identification of appropriate strategies. The student teachers also needed to recognise that the achievement of their learning goals was beneficial and worthwhile to their progress (outcome expectation) and that they would be able to persist in their efforts if faced with any difficulties.

One specific example from the findings was the expectation held by the visiting lecturers. The clarification from the student teachers on the relevance of their set learning goals, resulted in a specific goal focus. This factor was especially evident with one particular visiting lecturer, who asked student teachers at their initial meeting to consider whether their learning goal was challenging and appropriate enough for them. Self-selected goals are considered more challenging, prompting greater motivation and commitment (Zimmerman, 2008). The visiting lecturer specified that a challenging goal was more effective, because it directed the student teacher's attention to relevant behaviours, strategies and personal learning outcomes.

Self-regulated learners set goals in relation to extending their knowledge and sustaining their motivation, selecting strategies and monitoring their commitment to their goals, because goal setting on its own is not sufficient in becoming an adaptive expert (Timperley, 2011). At the initial practicum meetings between the visiting lecturers and student teachers, there was a discussion of what constitutes a high-quality goal. The criteria used for judging a high-quality goal, for the purposes of this chapter, were commitment, engagement, challenging and appropriate goals relevant to the student teachers' own learning.

During the performance monitoring phase of self-regulation, the visiting lecturers reinforced the student teachers' efforts, by assisting them to focus their attention on strategies and skills needed in order to achieve the goals and tasks set. The support and encouragement of both visiting lecturer and associate teacher was significant for student teachers as a catalyst for the improvement and progress of their goals. As Schunk (2001) commented, progress towards achieving goals "conveys to students they are capable of performing well, which enhances self-efficacy for continued learning" (p. 127). Close monitoring by both the visiting lecturer and associate teacher at this stage supported student teachers in the continued development of required skills, and there was the expectation that they could ask for assistance and guidance if necessary, at any time. When learners are confronted with challenging tasks and self-doubt, which might require the support of someone with more expertise, an important aspect of self-regulation is knowing when to revert to other-regulation, asking for input from others (Newman, 2008).

There are four levels of feedback questions in Hattie and Timperley's (2007) model of feedback. They are the task level, the process level, the self-regulation level and the self-level. Hattie and Timperley (2007) stated there is a distinction to be made between feedback about the task, about the processing of the task, about self-regulation, and feedback about the self. They argued that feedback about self is the least effective, feedback about self-regulation and feedback about the processing of the task are powerful in processing and mastery of tasks, and feedback about the task is powerful when the task information is useful for improving strategies or enhancing self-regulation (p. 91). Two of the levels are particularly pertinent to this chapter. One is the self-regulation level of self-monitoring, directing and regulating of actions, and the other level is the self-level of personal evaluations and affect (usually positive) on the learner.

During the performance monitoring phase, it was important that student teachers continued to monitor and be motivated in their performance towards the achievement of their learning goals. Two student teachers in the study commented on the constructive and specific feedback from their visiting lecturers which they received on the appropriateness and progress of their goals. They stated they used the feedback to make changes to their teaching and 'take action', and as a consequence critically reflect on the achievement of their goals and what they had learnt. Hattie and Timperley (2007) stated when feedback is drawn to the self-regulatory process which is needed to engage with a task, a learner then understands the importance of the effort needed and "their conceptions of learning can be important moderators in the learning process" (p. 102).

The evaluation of performance phase was also associated with the notion of student teachers maximising and accepting responsibility for their own learning through reflective practice. In one specific triadic/professional discussion, a student teacher signalled to the visiting lecturer and associate teacher, her ability to now make judgements about her performance, to know where she could alter and adjust her planning, and as a consequence was becoming more flexible and adaptable in her teaching practice. The visiting lecturer commented, in support of student teacher learning, it was about being willing and having the confidence to take risks in teaching which the student teacher was doing. The promotion of adaptive teaching expertise requires assistance from an expert who can "help novice student teachers learn from a highly complex and deeply contextualised learning process" (Soslau, 2012, p. 769).

Motivation plays an important part in the process of learning self-regulatory skills, through the learners' willingness to attempt challenging tasks, and deciding strategically on which approaches to utilise (Perry et al., 2008). Without motivation, self-regulated learning is more difficult to achieve (Zimmerman, 2008). With the support of the effective visiting lecturers and associate teachers, the student teachers displayed metacognitive skills, strategising the setting, monitoring and evaluating of their learning goals in relation to their strengths and weaknesses as learners, demonstrating motivation for the set task.

Implications for Policy and Practice

This chapter has implications for ITE and those associated with delivering policy in Faculties of Education and Universities now and in the future. Teaching student teachers is certainly demanding, because of the requirement to model practices, construct powerful learning experiences, support progress and practice, and to assess students and help link theory and practice (Bransford et al., 2005). A salient concern, however, is that, while initial teacher educators say they promote self-regulated learning, it is important that at an organisational level, the teaching of self-regulatory skills and practices to student teachers should not be left to chance and should be added to the above list of requirements.

However, for these self-regulatory skills to be promoted, both visiting lecturers and associate teachers need to see the value in student teachers learning these skills and providing the opportunities to develop and utilise them while on practicum. These skills need to be explicit and deliberately fostered by visiting lecturers and associate teachers committed to promoting self-regulation and goal setting, with their student teachers. If student teachers have experienced and practised the learning strategies of self-regulation and goal setting themselves, they are more likely to understand better the progress of the learners they teach (Tillema & Kremer-Hayon, 2002).

The three effective visiting lecturers succeeded in shifting the theoretical ideas underpinning the student teachers' self-regulatory skills into a reality of practice, within the high-stakes environment of practicum by monitoring the student teachers' progress, and supporting their learning constructively in partnership with the associate teacher. The complementary aspect of the partnership was particularly evident in the triadic/professional conversations when both visiting lecturers and associate teachers encouraged and promoted self-regulatory skills with student teachers. Just as students learn within their "zone of proximal development" supported by capable peers, student teachers learn more when supported by expert others (Hammerness et al., 2005).

The researcher acknowledges the significance of consciously shifting the perception of student teachers, to not merely passing the practicum, but also being about acquiring and learning self-regulatory skills. As indicated in this chapter, the skills of self-regulation are a crucial aspect of learning not only for student teachers but also for the learners they teach. Further, Zimmerman (2002) added that self-regulation is important, because one of the major functions of education is the development of life-long learning skills, and involves the self-awareness, self-motivation and behavioural skills and dispositions necessary to put that knowledge into practice.

Within the larger research study, there was variation in the quality of the effectiveness and the nature of the feedback given by the visiting lecturers and associate teachers to student teachers, in support of their learning. ITE should consider the aspects of pedagogical conversations that promote the strategies and skills of self-regulation, and consider ways student teachers can take responsibility for their own learning. Sustaining improvement in teaching and learning is dependent on student teachers developing professional, self-regulatory skills, using them to inquire into the effectiveness of their practice and continue to make adjustments to their practice (Timperley, 2008).

There were student teachers in the larger research study who did not have visiting lecturers supporting their learning through the development of self-regulation, to the same extent as three effective visiting lecturers reported in this chapter. It is to be noted though that all the student teachers reported in this chapter progressed and passed their practicum. However, it is problematic, and a matter of concern whether 'survival as such' by student teachers on practicum, and in their future in teaching is enough for the profession. Student teachers themselves need to have an awareness of being self-regulatory and the importance of developing those particular skills and behaviours. Without this rationale and real understanding, it is more than likely only superficial learning will occur.

Conclusion

What became evident based on this study was that the three visiting lecturers excelled in their role at supporting student teacher learning. Their explicit teaching of the skills of self-regulation, in turn, fostered the development of adaptive competence, an integral part of being an effective teacher. The three visiting lecturers were noticeably motivated by their desire to see the student teachers succeed and challenge themselves in their learning. However, ITE providers cannot rely on a random selection of visiting lecturers being motivated to change the practices of student teachers whom they visit on practicum and happen to have the skills to do so. There needs to be a greater engagement and motivation for visiting lecturers to explore their practice, and acquiring and improved knowledge and skill base to support students develop self-regulation during practicum. The incorporation of self-regulatory skills by visiting lecturers and associate teachers in partnership with each other, supporting student teachers and their learning should be a central part of any professional development programmes and be further explored in research and practice.

References

Bransford, J., Derry, S., Berliner, D., Hammerness, K., & Beckett, K. (2005). Theories of learning and their roles in teaching. In L. Darling-Hammond & J. Bransford (Eds.), *Preparing teachers for a changing world: What teachers should learn and be able to do* (pp. 40–87). San Francisco, CA: Jossey-Bass.

Buzza, D., Kotsopoulos, D., Mueller, J., & Johnston, M. (2013). Exploring the relationship between self-regulated learning and reflection in teacher education. *Journal of Teaching and Learning, 9*(1), 1–12. ISSN: 1911-8279.

Darling-Hammond, L., & Bransford, J. (Eds.) (with LePage, L., Hammerness, K., & Duffy, H.). (2005). *Preparing teachers for a changing world. What teachers should learn and be able to do.* San Francisco, CA: Jossey-Bass.

de Corte, E. (2010). Historical developments in the understanding of learning. In H. Dumont, D. Istance, & F. Benavides (Eds.), *The nature of learning: Using research to inspire practice.* Paris, France: OECD Publishing.

Donovan, S., Bransford, J., & Pellegrino, J. (2008). *How people learn. Bridging research and practice.* Washington, DC: National Academy Press.

Ezzy, D. (2002). *Qualitative analysis. Practice and innovation.* Sydney, NSW: Allen & Unwin.

Hammerness, K., Darling-Hammond, L., Bransford, J., Berliner, D., Cochran-Smith, M., McDonald, M., et al. (2005). How teachers learn and develop. In L. Darling-Hammond & J. Bransford (Eds.), *Preparing teachers for a changing world* (pp. 358–389). San Francisco, CA: Jossey-Bass.

Hattie, J. (2009). *Visible learning. A synthesis of over 800 meta-analyses relating to achievement.* New York, NY: Routledge.

Hattie, J., & Timperley, H. (2007). The power of feedback. *Review of Educational Research, 77*(1), 81–112.

Hiebert, J., Morris, A., Berk, D., & Jansen, A. (2007). Preparing teachers to learn from teaching. *Journal of Teacher Education, 58*(1), 47–61. https://doi.org/10.1177/0022487106295726.

Koerner, M., Rust, F., & Baumgartner, F. (2002). Exploring roles in student teaching placements. *Teacher Education Quarterly, 29*(2), 35–58.

Locke, E., & Latham, G. (2002). Building a practically useful theory of goal setting and task motivation. A 35-year odyssey. *American Psychologist, 57*(9), 705–717. https://doi.org/10.1037/0003-0066X57.9.705.

Newman, R. S. (2008). The motivational role of adaptive help seeking in self-regulated learning. In D. H. Schunk & B. J. Zimmerman (Eds.), *Motivation and self-regulated learning: Theory, research and applications* (pp. 315–337). New York, NY: Lawrence Erlbaum Associates.

Perry, N., Hutchinson, L., & Thauberger, C. (2008). Talking about teaching self-regulated learning: Scaffolding student teachers' development and use of practices that promote self-regulated learning. *International Journal of Educational Research, 47*(2), 97–108. https://doi.org/10.1016/j.ijer.2007.11.010.

Schunk, D. (2001). Social cognitive theory and self-regulated learning. In B. Zimmerman & D. Schunk (Eds.), *Self-regulated learning and academic achievement: Theoretical perspectives* (pp. 125–151). Mahwah, NJ: Lawrence Erlbaum Associates.

Soslau, E. (2012). Opportunities to develop adaptive teaching expertise during supervisory conferences. *Teachers and Teacher Education, 28*(5), 768–779. https://doi.org/10.1016/j.tate.2012.02.009.

Tillema, H., & Kremer-Hayon, L. (2002). "Practising what we preach"—teacher educators' dilemmas in promoting self-regulated learning: a cross case comparison. *Teaching and Teacher Education, 18*(5), 593–607.

Timperley, H. (2001). Mentoring converations designed to promote student teacher learning. *Asia-Pacific Journal of Teacher Education, 29*(2), 111–123.

Timperley, H. (2008). Teacher professional learning and development. In *Education Practices Series: Vol. 18*. Geneva, Switzerland: International Bureau of Education.

Timperley, H. (2011). The power of conversations: Developing adaptive expertise through the analysis of practice. *Monograph Submitted to the International Congress for School Effectiveness and School Improvement.*

Tschannen-Moran, M. (2001). The interconnectivity of trust in schools. In D. V. Maele, M. V. Houtte, & P. Forsyth (Eds.), *Trust and school life. The role of trust for learning, teaching, leading and bridging* (pp. 57–82). New York, NY: Springer.

Williams, J. (2014). Teacher educator professional learning in the third space: Implications for identity and practice. *Journal of Teacher Education, 65*(4), 315–332. https://doi.org/10.1177/0022487114533128.

Winne, P. H., & Hadwin, A. F. (2008). The weave of motivation and self-regulated learning. In D. H. Schunk & B. J. Zimmerman (Eds.), *Motivation and self-regulated learning: Theory, research and applications* (pp. 297–314). Mahwah, NJ: Lawrence Erlbaum Associates.

Zimmerman, B. J. (2000). Attaining self-regulation: A social cognitive perspective. In M. Boekaerts, P. Pintrich, & M. Zeidner (Eds.), *Handbook of self-regulation* (pp. 13–35). San Diego, CA: Academic Press.

Zimmerman, B. J. (2002). Becoming a self-regulated learner. *Theory into Practice, 41*(2), 64–70.

Zimmerman, B. J. (2008). Goal setting: A key proactive source of academic self-regulation. In D. H. Schunk & B. J. Zimmerman (Eds.), *Motivation and self-regulated learning: Theory, research and applications* (pp. 267–295). New York, NY: Lawrence Erlbaum Associates.

Author Biography

Lyn McDonald is a Senior Lecturer at the Faculty of Education and Social Work at the University of Auckland. Her research interests include the practicum (professional experience), student teacher learning while on practicum and the role the visiting lecturer (university teacher educator) plays in that learning. Her role as an initial teacher educator and visiting lecturer has taken Lyn into a large number of New Zealand primary and intermediate school classrooms and enabled her to work with, and alongside, many student teachers and associate teachers (mentor teachers). This is an area which she enjoys, visiting student teachers while on practicum and the partnerships she establishes with schools. The second body of research she has been involved in is the role as senior researcher in an externally funded empirical research project 2011–14 (awarded $300,000 from the Marsden fund) entitled 'Teacher Expectations: an intervention study' from which there have been many publications.

Chapter 8
Preparing Teachers to Work with and for Remote Indigenous Communities: Unsettling Institutional Practices

Jennifer Rennie, Simone White, Peter Anderson and Anna Darling

Abstract This chapter reports on data from two separate Australian Government-funded projects related to the development of a remote professional experience. The first project, PREEpared (https://www.preepared.com) was interested in finding ways to better prepare pre-service teachers and teacher educators to counter oppressive curriculum and pedagogy and work with and for Australian remote communities in the context of Initial Teacher Education (ITE). The second involved planning, implementing and evaluating two remote placement experiences to understand the experiences of all relevant stakeholders. The question of how can ITE best serve remote communities was posed and a themed analysis conducted from a range of interview responses. Findings suggest those in initial teacher education need to unsettle some of the taken-for-granted professional education practices and documents the essential elements of a curriculum necessary to prepare pre-service teachers to work and learn in ethical, respectful and reciprocal ways. Analysis suggests that a specialised initial teacher education curriculum and professional experience that acknowledges and respects local needs and contexts is needed to adequately prepare teachers to work in and for remote communities where it is difficult to both attract and retain teachers.

Keywords Professional experience · Remote placement
Initial teacher education · Indigenous education · Pre-service teachers

J. Rennie (✉) · A. Darling
Monash University, Melbourne, VIC, Australia
e-mail: jennifer.rennie@monash.edu

A. Darling
e-mail: anna.darling@monash.edu

S. White · P. Anderson
Queensland University of Technology, Brisbane, QLD, Australia
e-mail: simone.white@qut.edu.au

P. Anderson
e-mail: p21.anderson@qut.edu.au

© Springer Nature Singapore Pte Ltd. 2018
D. Heck and A. Ambrosetti (eds.), *Teacher Education In and For Uncertain Times*,
https://doi.org/10.1007/978-981-10-8648-9_8

Introduction

Just over one quarter of the Aboriginal and Torres Strait Islander population in Australia reside in remote or very remote locations (ABS, 2011) with the majority of schools in remote areas having Indigenous enrolments greater than 90%. Whilst the definition of 'remoteness' can be subjective, generally, 'remote' is classified with regard to ease of distance and access to a variety of amenities of comfort, as well as distance to major towns and cities; Whilst 'very remote' would constitute a larger degree of hardship in accessing these amenities, as well as living extraordinarily far from major cities and towns (Wakerman, 2004). These geographically isolated but culturally rich communities often face teacher shortages, creating further a level of uncertainty for ensuring access to educational opportunity for those who live and work in these places.

This chapter discusses how initial teacher education providers might best address the current remote staffing issues Whilst also meeting the challenge set for universities by the Indigenous Cultural Competency Reform in Australian universities report to ensure all graduates are well equipped to work in culturally competent ways with Indigenous communities (DEEWR, 2011, p. 9). The authors, as a team of Indigenous and non-Indigenous teacher education researchers, explored this policy imperative and staffing concern, from the perspective of initial teacher education and the preparation of graduates to work with and for Indigenous remote contexts, as just one example of turning policy into practice. A particular focus on curriculum design and developing a culturally responsive remote professional experience were explored as a way to interrogate initial teacher education institutional practices that would best serve remote communities. What this work to date has uncovered is the fraught and uncertain nature of policy reform and enactment and the importance of building strong partnerships between Indigenous communities and initial teacher education that reflect the learning needs of Aboriginal and Torres Strait Islander students first.

Exploring Higher Education Policy and Practice

Higher education is awash with important policy imperatives ranging from those designed to improve access and opportunity for all students, to government-imposed initial teacher education standards and accreditation. As raised earlier, one of the driving overarching recommendations of the Indigenous Cultural Competency Reform in Australian universities (2011) project has aimed for all university graduates to 'have the knowledge and skills necessary to interact in a culturally competent way with Indigenous communities' (DEEWR, 2011, p. 9). Where this knowledge base is embedded into initial teacher education curriculum becomes the next challenge.

Likewise, the Australian Institute of Teaching and School Leadership (AITSL) names specific standards for teachers to meet as they relate to Aboriginal and Torres

Strait Islander students and culture. Specifically the 1.4 and 2.4 standards state that all graduate teachers should be able to 'Demonstrate broad knowledge and understanding of the impact of culture, cultural identity and linguistic background on the education of students from Aboriginal and Torres Strait Islander backgrounds', and 'Demonstrate broad knowledge of, understanding of and respect for Aboriginal and Torres Strait Islander histories, cultures and languages' (AITSL, 2017). These standards have challenged universities and schools alike in terms of how to build teacher cultural awareness and understanding of the standards and initial teacher education providers' response to the accreditation documentation.

Further to these policy directions is the need for all ITE providers to demonstrate mandated partnerships as part of new accreditation requirements. This policy direction is complicated by schools who are increasingly finding it difficult to accommodate pre-service teachers due to their own increasing accountability and testing requirements. In response, many universities are looking at alternative and international professional experiences (where pre-service teachers often subsidise their own travel) to ensure all pre-service teachers are placed. Remote placements, as a result, are often advertised alongside international professional experience as an 'alternative' placement. Building professional experience programmes with remote schools has therefore been an area of expansion to meet the standards, and there has now begun some research into the challenges and opportunities in doing so. However, the majority of research as reported (Baills, Bell, Greensill, & Wilcox, 2002) focuses on the logistics of setting up professional experiences, and there are similarities here in findings from rural professional experiences studies (Kline, White, & Lock, 2013). Such studies highlight interrelating issues such as placement planning and coordinating, financial expense, geographical isolation and challenges of finding suitable accommodation for pre-service teachers (Sharplin, 2002; Yarrow, Ballantyne, Hansford, Herschell, & Millwater, 1999).

There remains a paucity of the impact and consequences of remote professional experiences from the various stakeholders working in and with remote communities. Policy tends to focus on mandated 'partnerships' (Teacher Education Ministerial Advisory Group, 2014) but it is unclear what such partnerships look like 'in' and 'for' remote communities. Herbert (2007) cautions that relationship work is foundational to developing partnerships with Indigenous communities. Relationship work requires honesty and involves making an unwritten agreement 'to listen', and 'to reflect' on what is said 'within the framework of your own understandings' (p. 47).

Many universities (mostly based in urban settings) have attempted to develop 'remote' professional experiences to allow pre-service teachers the opportunity to experience and learn more about remote schools and communities in the hope that this experience will instil a remote-teaching mindset and increase the likelihood of a remote-teaching career. Whilst at first glance this type of initiative appears positive, there is the real danger that if not carefully co-developed with local community and schools leading the initiative, the experience can end up being a type of 'edutourism' (Hickling-Hudson & Alquist, 2003) which can in turn lead to unintended negative consequences for Indigenous learners. More recently, the work of establishing remote professional experiences has been named as 'dangerous practices' by

Auld, Dyer, and Charles (2016). They explain that by dangerous they mean 'those practices at risk of being counterproductive to the empowering and transformative practices of student learning and the ethical responsibilities associated with teaching' (p. 165). The question of how to best prepare teachers to work in remote contexts further challenges institutions to think differently about how they build professional experiences and cultural responsiveness for pre-service teachers *without* unwittingly causing a negative impact for Indigenous communities.

The Study: Drawing on Two Remote Professional Experience Projects

It is within this vexed policy and practice backdrop that this chapter reports findings drawn from a dataset across two Australian Government-funded projects aimed to investigate the development of remote placement experiences. The first project, an Office of Learning and Teaching seed project now known as Partnering for Remote Education Experience or PREEpared (https://www.preepared.com), was interested in finding ways to better prepare pre-service teachers and teacher educators to counter oppressive curriculum and pedagogy and work with and for remote communities in the context of ITE from the perspective of teacher educators. The second project funded by Federal Government Indigenous Advancement Strategy involved planning, implementing and evaluating two remote placement experiences to understand them from the perspectives of the communities and schools. Together these projects offer new ways of understanding how universities can do this work so they might reduce the level of uncertainty and risk for remote communities and schools. To begin to address some of these uncertainties, the research teams posed the question from both projects—how can universities reconceptualise culturally responsive institutional practices around the development and implementation of remote placements?

Each project was theoretically firmly underpinned by the *United Nations Declaration on the Rights of Indigenous Peoples* (United Nations, 2008), of which Australia is a signatory. This document provides a framework to address the collective and individual rights of First Nations peoples to education along with other key areas of need. This informs the practices of rights-based education and pedagogy for First Nations peoples. This approach is guided by 'a different set of questions' (Smith, 1999, p. 94) that prioritise and frame Indigenous approaches to education and pedagogy as self-determining and rights-based.

Secondly, the projects were informed by the International Labour Organisation's Convention 169 on Indigenous and Tribal Peoples (ILO 169), which, in the context of education and rights-based pedagogy, speaks to Indigenous peoples' right to education in terms of contribution to society and self-determination (Ma Rhea & Anderson, 2011). The aims of Indigenous rights-based education are expressed in rights-based pedagogy through the creation of curriculum and pedagogic approaches that advocate for 'education for consciousness-raising' (Falcon & Jacob, 2011, p. 26). These approaches have underpinned the project's recommendations for the collaborative facilitation of remote-teaching placements. The qualitative research methodology was explicitly underscored by Indigenous and Indigenist research methodologies that 'privileged the Indigenous voice' (Hogarth, 2017, p. 24). Data arising from the interviews were analysed using the process of identifying and coding characteristic patterns or themes emerging (Braun & Clarke, 2006; Creswell, 2009).

Both studies used interviews as the primary means of data collection to try and understand the experiences of various stakeholders within the space of 'remote placement'. Ethics was gained by Monash University for both projects. Data were collected in 2016. As part of the Office of Learning and Teaching funded project (Project 1), seven interviews with Indigenous and non-Indigenous teacher educators and education experts with substantial experience in facilitating remote-teaching placements were conducted over a period of six months to gain a sense of their experiences of doing this work (Project 1). In the same year, fifteen interviews were conducted with Principals, Indigenous and Non-Indigenous teachers and pre-service teachers about their experiences of developing, experiencing and sustaining remote placement experiences (Project 2). The data presented is identified according to the role and which project it was sourced. Utilising data from both projects has enabled the collective research team to present a balanced view of the experiences of all those involved in this important work.

Transcripts from each of the groups interviewed were analysed using an inductive process, based on assumptions of interpretive qualitative research (Guba & Lincoln, 1981). Common themes were identified about what each group thought was important for the planning and implementation of this work. Constant and comparative analysis of the data developed a set of inductive categories that emerged by sorting the data into key themes. The following presents a discussion of these findings.

Discussion

The combined study revealed that there were a number of important considerations in relation to establishing the remote experience; the curriculum that prepares pre-service teachers for the experience before, during and after the placement and what relationship building might mean within this context for the remote professional experience. Whilst these are key aspects to focus on in creating a remote placement, what also emerged from the study was that particular institutional practices governing professional experience need to be interrogated and adjusted. At the heart of this work is the importance of building relationships and partnerships with the local community first, and the recognition that Indigenous learners need to come before the desires of pre-service teachers to experience a remote-teaching placement. A closer look at the emerging themes is now discussed.

Building Trust and Partnership: Getting It 'Rights-Based'

Building trust and a partnership that values Indigenous learners and learning emerged as a key theme. Data revealed different approaches to establishing remote placement opportunities. Despite these differences, all of the participants talked about the ongoing issues associated with finding the 'right' place for teacher education students. These included establishing partnerships with education departments and schools in other jurisdictions, accessibility, accommodation, financial considerations, the experience of mentor teachers, pastoral care for pre-service teachers and timing of the placement. In particular, universities wanted to partner with schools where the students were well supported, safe and had opportunities for rich learning experiences.

Whilst there was an emphasis on finding the 'right' place for students from the university perspective, all community stakeholders, Principals, teachers and schools talked about the importance of the 'right' student. Both school Principals and most of the teachers from Project 2 expressed a level of uncertainty around whether they would be sent the 'right' student to their school and community. By right, they meant culturally responsive. They frequently used words and phrases such as 'knowing their stuff', being 'culturally aware', the ability to 'build relationships with students, parents and community', 'resilient', 'resourcefulness' and being 'healthy' emotionally.

All of the teachers and Principals emphasised the importance of sending pre-service teachers who were well prepared, culturally aware and had a level of resilience and resourcefulness. The importance of this is echoed in research (Warren & Quine, 2013). This is important as these communities are challenging places in which to work. Teachers have to cope with cultural, professional and geographical isolation, language and cultural barriers, and limited resources (Lock, Budgen, Lunay, & Oakley, 2012). Those interviewed were clear that not having the 'right' student can be a challenge for these schools, as the following data from an interview with a Principal about a recent placement experience show,

> I found these students seemed really prepared, open minded or able to roll with it. We do have students who come up here and it's not very successful. It's clunky and these guys haven't been like that at all they've been really open minded and they've also been pretty proactive. (Principal, Project 2)

These sentiments were also echoed by three of the teacher educators interviewed. One remarked how sending a pre-service teacher who is not the right fit can negatively affect both the community and the school.

> But, it can all go downhill very, very fast and while a lot of people see the difficulty and the destabilisation that occurs with a teacher who might go in and not be able to cope, often the effect on the community, of teacher upon teacher upon teacher can be huge. (Teacher Educator, Project 1)

Whilst it is not uncommon for pre-service teachers in any given professional experience to have issues in schools they are placed, it was clear from the data that this presented particular unwanted challenges for remote schools and communities. The tyranny of distance also means that it is much more difficult for universities to intervene and solve issues that might arise. Universities that had remote placement as a regular offering in remote schools talked about the importance of placing pre-service teachers as a team and the need for students to go through a selection process to try and ensure they sent the 'right' students. This included students submitting a written application that addressed a set of criteria followed by an interview process. Whilst this was not reported as being 'fool proof', feedback from both schools involved said that students from universities which 'selected students' were often easier to work with. Universities then would need to allow time for a selection process that allows them to ensure that they are sending the 'right' students to these community schools which as detailed earlier are often 'high needs schools' with a number of challenges of their own (Price, 2016). This practice requires that universities work differently from the taken-for-granted practices of placing individual students with a mentor in a school. It requires pedagogical work of building a relationship with a remote school community and then a process of selection of pre-service teachers rather than 'all pre-service teachers are placed and given permission to go'. It is acknowledged that the vetting of pre-service teachers (especially those who are prepared to subsidise their own experience) can cause issues for placement officers. Traditionally, placement officers prioritise placing all pre-service teachers and vetting changes their work to one where they are not only required to adopt a cohort model of placement but also to value the right of the school to select rather than the right of the student to be placed.

Building the Knowledge Base First: The Importance of Curriculum Before Practice

Moreton-Robinson et al. (2012) identified the paucity of Indigenous content in Australian ITE programmes; this was further echoed in practice by Ma Rhea, Anderson, and Atkinson (2012) who found that the majority of teachers in Australia were not confident to teach Aboriginal and Torres Strait Islander content with any depth or rigour. Thus, perpetuating the stereotypical learned curriculum taught in ITE programmes. All of the teacher educators and pre-service teachers talked about the importance of specific units within education courses that addressed historical and contemporary issues related to Aboriginal and Torres Strait Islander peoples and effective pedagogies for working with Indigenous students and about the importance of developing culturally competent students. Further, all stakeholders interviewed discussed the need for induction programmes both before and during the placement.

University teacher educators discussed offering several units within their courses that explored various issues around Indigenous education both within the Faculty of Education and other faculties. These units aimed to develop a broad knowledge, understanding and respect for Indigenous peoples, histories, culture and languages, explore a range of Indigenous perspectives on teaching and learning and develop the skills and insights to engage learners from Indigenous and traditional communities and create partnerships to improve learning outcomes. However, how and when these units were offered varied greatly. In some institutions, they were compulsory units as part of an Education degree whereas in other institutions, students elected to take the units. Further, there was no consistency in the years in which they occurred during the degree.

Unanimously, all teacher educators that were interviewed highlighted the importance of all students undertaking a unit that developed their cultural competence and explored issues around Indigenous perspectives on teaching and learning whether or not they wanted to explore a remote placement. Further, they felt it was important to challenge and unsettle their assumptions about Indigenous culture and knowledge more generally. One teacher educator commented,

> Personally I start with who they are, and where they form their values from where they get their stereo-types from, where they get their values of who they are, why they wanted to become a teacher in the first place and their interest being wanting to go to a rural remote or an Aboriginal community or work with indigenous students. (Teacher educator, Project 1)

Some also suggested that one unit does not go far enough and that university courses should give much more emphasis to a curriculum that firmly embeds Indigenous perspectives on teaching and learning across all unit offerings. One participant suggested that we should start early in the course so that students can start thinking about whether they might like to pursue options for placement in remote Indigenous contexts early in their degree as the following data show,

> I am wondering whether rural and remote and embedding of Indigenous perspectives, should be clearly outlined in their first year so that the student can start mapping, 'If I want to do this, should I look at taking up an Indigenous studies minor so I can get my head around the kids of knowledges I need to know before I get into a setting like this. Should I get myself into these sorts of units?' (Teacher educator, Project 1)

These sentiments were also echoed from pre-service teachers (Project 2). An Indigenous pre-service teacher made the following comments in a conversation where she was asked how prepared she felt to do this work. She commented,

> I am not the slightest bit concerned. I think having grown up in an Indigenous background it is an advantage in knowing what to expect. In terms of my degree I don't think my university has prepared me adequately I think it was somewhat helpful in relation to why we need to integrate Indigenous perspectives into planning etc. But none of my other units have really done anything … I am still in classes with people who have racist or prejudice or really oblivious views. I think university education needs to challenge that from the get go. I don't know how to fix it but we need to challenge those perspectives. (Pre-service teacher, Project 2)

Further responses seemed to suggest that the greatest priority was related to prospective students having an understanding of 'their community' rather than more general issues that were covered in the units offered by universities. There was a real sense that an induction process that was specific to their schools and their community was considered important.

Connecting Curriculum and Remote Professional Experience

It was clear throughout the data that an induction process before pre-service teachers embark on a remote-teaching placement is necessary. Moreover, all participants talked about the importance of developing this in consultation with both school and community so that it can be tailored specifically to their needs. Again, how these induction programmes work varied across institutions regarding content and delivery. Some talked about preparing booklets, others about having formal induction face-to-face session, and others talked about a combination of ways.

> We have over the years built up, I think, quite a substantial induction program. We have a face-to-face and an online induction for the students beforehand, and we work with an Aboriginal Elder in developing them and delivering that program. The students, even though it's not compulsory, we encourage them to come and they find that very useful. So yes, we have built up a suite of activities. And also we use the RRR, the Reconciliation, Respect and Relationships website now also. (Teacher educator Project 1)

Despite this, some suggested that whilst you can go through a process of induction with students before they leave 'you can never prepare students a hundred per cent for such an experience' (Principal, Project 2). When schools were asked about induction processes they said they also liked to have students go through a process of induction when they arrive. This included things such as showing them around the community and school, going through 'don't go areas', discussing appropriate behaviour and dress, and safety issues. Further staff interviewed at the two schools who participated in this study said they often invited students to be part of other activities that would help them to better understand the cultural aspects of living and working in their community. For example, students in one school were invited to go on the 'Learning on Country' camp implemented by the Language and Culture team at the school.

It was clear throughout the data that the remote placement can be a rich learning experience. University educators and pre-service teachers alike talked about the benefits.

> Well I think the positives are, first of all, that you are providing opportunities for students that they wouldn't normally have, so that it is extending their vision and their sense of understanding about Australia in terms of seeing through the lens of Aboriginal history and Aboriginal reconciliation. I think it actually prompts and promotes that critical and often uncomfortable enquiry into our history and into our sense of reconciliation between white and black Australia. (Teacher educator, Project 1)

Similarly, both Principals talked about the benefits in relation to future recruitment of teachers and in teacher learning at their school. One commented:

> But I see it as the most important thing for us, is that yes, it's a great recruiting tool. I think it's paying back to the fact that we need to do that to build great teachers, to have good mentor teachers to work with teachers, but I also see it as our teachers having to reflect on their practice. And I think that's really important. Explain their practice, demonstrate their practice, have somebody probably give them some feedback in a roundabout way about what they did, because they're asking questions—why did you do that? And they have to explain—I did it for this reason. (Principal, Project 2)

Despite the potential for remote placements to be sites of rich learning, interviews with Principals and teachers suggest that there needs to be a level of flexibility regarding what is possible. Often universities have already prepared unit guides detailing what pre-service teachers are required to do such as addressing various teaching standards and planning and implementing a minimum number of learning experiences. These are often being driven by teacher standards and registration requirements. There is a need to negotiate and collaborate with schools regarding the learning that might be possible. So rather than taking a pre-determined set of learning requirements to the school, we should be asking what is possible within that context.

The importance of relationship building was evident throughout the various data. To set up the placement, there is a great deal of brokerage with education departments, schools and local communities.

> The difficulties of facilitating a remote area placement is if someone who hadn't done this before came in, it's about building relationships with departments, with the schools, so that's why it's a long term thing and that's why there always needs to be someone who's in the wings, who knows the program, who we've got for succession planning. So I guess what I'm saying is it's not as straightforward as a normal placement. (Teacher educator, Project 1)

Further, there was the sense that you had to have succession planning in place to ensure that the relationships were sustainable. It was also clear throughout all of the data that this 'relationship' work was somehow different and more complex than what we might be accustomed to.

> Building the relationship locks in such a western, liberal, humanistic idea of simplistic friendship, and I think building a relationship with communities is just very, very different. And, what that means, I think is that the universities have to take responsibility for building very strong community relationships, which then means they're very clear about the conditions under which their pre-service teachers go to the community. So, it's not about—on the one hand it is about friendship, but on the other it's about deep, deep political and cultural knowledge. (Teacher educator, Project 1)

It was also strongly evident that this relationship building takes a considerable amount of time and that it involves a collaborative exercise where the community and schools have a real investment in how the partnership and placement experience is developed and implemented as one teacher educator explains below.

> Aboriginal communities are very, there's a lot of fly-in, fly-out people that are continually coming through Aboriginal communities without proper negotiation with the Elders of the group, and what really works. So the two worlds aren't communicating, everyone has their job to do, so I think we need to do the consultation process better, and it should be driven from the communities, not the other way around. So the communities should have a say in what happens and what kind of preparation the student's need to have before going out to their placements, in their schools, on their community, because we don't prepare them for that (Teacher educator, Project 1).

All of the Principals and teachers interviewed also emphasised the importance of developing the relationship with both the school and the community. Further, they said that it was also important for pre-service teachers to be mindful of doing this work whilst they are in their schools. One teacher commented on the importance of relationship building with students for learning.

It really is experience and it really is breaking down and going through the hardship and coming up because so much of the learning is relationship building. For these kids to teach literacy and numeracy a good relationship is the foundation. (Teacher, Project 2)

The data suggest a real need for universities to engender the importance of this work from the initial organisation through to the enactment of the placement experience. Further, we should ensure that teacher educators and pre-service teachers alike are involved in this work.

Implications: Creating More Certainty?

Appropriate preparation of pre-service teachers for remote professional experience and the formation and maintenance of strong, long-term relationships between universities and remote schools and communities appears to be at the heart of the sustainability of remote-teaching placements. As such we need to unsettle some of the taken-for-granted practices around the establishment, development and maintenance of the university—school partnership. In addition to having the interests of students at heart, universities also need to ensure that they are meeting the needs of the communities and schools. Partnerships need to be reciprocal. Data from the various stakeholders suggest that there is an enormous amount of work that goes into the initial stages of setting up the partnership and planning for a remote placement. Allowing enough time to develop and plan these experiences would seem paramount. Most importantly ensuring that there are processes in place to ensure that schools and communities are considered by sending the 'right' teacher education student and that students are considered by choosing the 'right' place.

To do this, there needs to be a level of 'certainty' around the processes for student selection and schools need some reassurance that these processes will be maintained. Arguably, sending 'anyone' to these communities and schools as the data clearly shows how this can be 'risky' and unsettling for communities and schools alike. Further practices need to be put in place to ensure the maintenance and further development of these relationships so the 'fly in fly out' syndrome that has plagued these schools and communities for decades can be avoided. In the development of the partnership, a great deal of flexibility is required. The taken-for-granted institutional placement practices do not work in these places. There needs to be a process of negotiation around what is possible regarding student learning. So rather than saying this is what students need to do, we need to ask what is possible?

Finally, creating more opportunities for a remote placement 'to schools with high Indigenous student populations can empower and professionally enhance the effectiveness of learning and teaching to their students' (Harrington, 2013, p. 87). As evidenced by the data, it can also assist pre-service teachers in making decisions about future career possibilities in these communities and schools which can work towards addressing uncertainty around staffing. However, the issue of appropriate preparation before and during the placement remains crucial. Partington (2003) warns that 'ignorance of Indigenous history, oppression, culture and expectations is likely to lead teachers to adopt strategies that compound the disadvantages Indigenous students experience and accelerate their departure from school' (p. 40). Thus, institutions tasked with the responsibility to prepare pre-service teachers for the remote placement 'need to expose their students to the significant, broad and complex issues relevant to rural, regional and remote education' (Trinidad et al., 2011, p. 41). All of the participants in both projects agreed that a dedicated curriculum that addressed historical and contemporary issues related to Aboriginal and Torres Strait Islander peoples and effective pedagogies for working with Indigenous students and about the importance of developing culturally competent students was a necessary prerequisite for pre-service teachers wishing to embark on a remote placement. Further that a process of induction relevant to working in the community and school was necessary both before and during the placement. This again requires we unsettle the taken-for-granted practices of doing this work.

Conclusion

In conclusion, the findings from this study have a number of implications for the implementation of various policy requirements including the development of mandated partnerships (TEMAG, 2014), ensuring that graduates have the knowledge and skills to interact with Indigenous communities in culturally competent ways (DEEWR, 2011) and that they meet standards 1.4 and 2.4 for the purpose of accreditation (AITSL, 2017). First, developing partnerships with Indigenous remote communities requires we re-examine how universities work with Indigenous communities. The traditional approach of placing a pre-service teacher with a classroom teacher does not work for remote contexts—rather the 'placement' needs to be viewed as a partnership between the university, community and school. Partnership building requires time, flexibility, trust and reciprocity.

Secondly, ensuring Indigenous learners are at the fore means that all pre-service teachers need to build their cultural responsive knowledge base first through a core curriculum which specifically addresses standards 1.4 and 2.4. Students who demonstrate their cultural responsiveness and awareness should then be offered a remote placement. ITE can do more to build the partnership between the curriculum and the remote professional experience, and placement officers and academic staff need to work together to build an Indigenous rights-based model.

Remote placements can indeed become a window into future opportunities to teach in remote settings for pre-service teachers, provided the collaborative induction process is thorough, and the main stakeholders are well supported and resourced. A remote professional experience, which for many students is a one-off experience (however transformative), may not be enough to entice these educators to teach in remote schools long-term and can unwittingly contribute to the staffing churn with a negative impact on student learning. This practice needs to be stopped.

As the alternative, the creation of specialist remote-teaching programmes and/or units needs to be undertaken as part of undergraduate and/or postgraduate teaching degrees. Also, the emphasis on curriculum should be broadened beyond a narrow focus on content and pedagogic knowledge, to include issues of preparation and planning before, during and post-placement, foregrounding the complex and interacting issues of the 'right' motivations to undertake the placement and relationship building with Indigenous communities. Ultimately, any improvements need to be undertaken with the explicit involvement of Indigenous remote school Principals, schools and communities. The invaluable feedback from these stakeholders, when placed at the heart of teacher education courses, pre- and post-remote placement support, could result in better outcomes for Indigenous students.

References

Auld, G., Dyer, J., & Charles, C. (2016). Dangerous practices: The practicum experiences of non-Indigenous pre-service teachers in remote communities. *Australian Journal of Teacher Education, 41*(6), 165–179.

Australian Bureau of Statistics. (2011). *Estimates of aboriginal and torres strait islander Australians* (Cat. No 3238.0.55.001). Canberra, Australia: ABS. Retrieved from http://www.abs.gov.au/ausstats/abs@.nsf/mf/3238.0.55.001.

Australian Institute for Teaching and School Leadership (AITSL). (2017). *Australian professional standards for teachers*. Retrieved from https://www.aitsl.edu.au/teach/standards.

Baills, L., Bell, S., Greensill, B., & Wilcox, L. (2002). Bridging the gap between beginning teachers and isolated/rural communities. *Education in Rural Australia, 12*(1), 55–62.

Braun, V., & Clarke, V. (2006). Using thematic analysis in psychology. *Qualitative Research in Psychology, 3*(2), 77–101.

Creswell, J. (2009). *Research design: Qualitative, quantitative and mixed methods approaches* (3rd ed.). Thousand Oaks, CA: Sage.

Department Education, Employment and Workplace Relations (DEEWR). (2011). *Guiding principles for developing Indigenous cultural competency in Australian universities*. Retrieved from https://www.universitiesaustralia.edu.au/uni-participation-quality/Indigenous-Higher-Education/Indigenous-Cultural-Compet#.WbX9BIc0Mbw.

Falcon, S. M., & Jacob, M. M. (2011). Human rights pedagogies in the classroom: Social justice, US Indigenous communities, and CSL projects. *Societies Without Borders, 6*(2), 23–50.

Guba, E., & Lincoln, Y. (1981). *Effective evaluation*. San Francisco, CA: Jossey-Bass.

Harrington, I. (2013). When the wattle comes out, the turtles are ready: Success of the enhanced teacher training program. *Australian Journal of Teacher Education, 38*(5), 80–88.

Herbert, J. (2007). Partnerships, pathways and policies: Improving Indigenous education outcomes. *Ngoonjook, 31*, 45–57.

Hickling-Hudson, A., & Ahlquist, R. (2003). Contesting the curriculum in the schooling of Indigenous children in Australia and the United States: From Eurocentrism to culturally powerful pedagogies. *Comparative Education Review, 47*(1), 64–89.

Hogarth, M. (2017). Speaking back to the deficit discourse: A theoretical and methodological approach. *Australian Educational Research, 44*(1), 21–34.

Kline, J., White, S., & Lock, G. (2013). The rural practicum: Preparing a quality teacher workforce for rural and regional Australia. *Journal of Research in Rural Education, 28*(3), 1–13.

Lock, G., Budgen, F., Lunay, R., & Oakley, G. (2012). Welcome to the outback: The paradoxes of living and teaching in remote Western Australian schools. *Australian and International Journal of Rural Education, 22*(3), 117–134.

Ma Rhea, Z., & Anderson, P. (2011). Economic justice and Indigenous education: Assessing the potential of standards-based and progressive education under ILO169. *Social Alternatives, 30*(4), 25–31.

Ma Rhea, Z., Anderson, P. J., & Atkinson, B. (2012). *National professional standards for teachers standards 1.4 and 2.4: Improving teaching in aboriginal and torres strait islander education.* Melbourne: AITSL. Retrieved from https://www.aitsl.edu.au/docs/default-source/default-document-library/improving-teaching-in-aboriginal-and-torres-strait-islander-education-professional-development-and-the-australian-professional-standards-for-teachers-monash-university.pdf?sfvrsn=55e7ec3c_0.

Moreton-Robinson, A. M., Singh, D., Kolopenuk, J., Robinson, A., & Walter, M. (2012). *Learning the lessons? Pre-service teacher preparation for teaching aboriginal and torres strait islander students.* A Report prepared for the Division of Indigenous Education and Training Futures–Queensland Department of Education, Training and Employment, Indigenous Studies Research Network, Queensland University of Technology.

Partington, G. (2003). Why Indigenous issues are an essential component of teacher education programs. *Australian Journal of Teacher Education, 27*(2), 39–48.

Price, K. (2016). More aboriginal and torres strait islander teachers for Australian high-needs schools. In J. Lampert & B. Burnett (Eds.), *Teacher education for high poverty schools* (pp. 95–114). Switzerland: Springer International Publishing. https://doi.org/10.1007/978-3-319-22059-8_6.

Sharplin, E. (2002). A taste of country: A pre-service teacher rural field trip. *Education in Rural Australia, 20*(1), 17–23.

Smith, L. T. (1999). *Decolonising methodologies: Research and Indigenous practices.* Dunedin, NZ: University of Otago Press.

Teacher Education Ministerial Advisory Group (TEMAG). (2014). *Action now: Classroom ready teachers.* Canberra: Australian Government. Retrieved from https://www.aitsl.edu.au/tools-resources/resource/action-now-classroom-ready-teachers-australian-government-response.

Trinidad, S., Sharplin, E., Lock, G., Ledger, S., Boyd, D., & Terry, E. (2011). Developing strategies at the pre-service level to address critical teacher attraction and retention issues in Australian rural, regional and remote schools. *Education in Rural Australia, 21*(1), 111–120.

United Nations. (2008). *Declaration on the rights of Indigenous peoples.* Retrieved from http://www.un.org/esa/socdev/unpfii/documents/DRIPS_en.pdf.

Wakerman, J. (2004). Defining remote health. *Australian Journal of Rural Health, 12*(5), 210–214.

Warren, E., & Quine, J. (2013). A holistic approach to supporting the learning of young Indigenous students: One case study. *The Australian Journal of Indigenous Education, 42*(1), 12–23.

Yarrow, A., Ballantyne, R., Hansford, B., Herschell, P., & Millwater, J. (1999). Teaching in rural and remote schools: A literature review. *Teaching and Teacher Education, 15,* 1–13.

Author Biographies

Jennifer Rennie is a Senior Lecturer in literacy education in the Faculty of Education, Monash University. Before working in higher education, she worked for several years as a primary and high school teacher. Her research interests relate to indigenous literacy, students who are marginalised from mainstream schooling and reading pedagogy for struggling and disengaged adolescent readers. Her recent research involves a project funded by the Collier Foundation that involves working with young mothers who have returned to education and a project funded by the Office for Learning and Teaching that involves developing a set of protocols for engaging with remote indigenous communities when planning and implementing placement opportunities for pre-service teachers. She has published widely in the area of Indigenous literacy and reading.

She is a Principal Fellow with the Australian Literacy Educators Association and has been the Managing Editor of the Australian Journal of Language and Literacy since 2009.

Simone White is Professor and Assistant Dean (International and Engagement) in the Faculty of Education at Queensland University of Technology (QUT). She is also the Immediate Past President of the Australian Teacher Education Association (ATEA). Her publications, research and teaching are focused on the key question of how to best prepare teachers and leaders for diverse communities (both local and global). Her current research areas focus on teacher education policy, teacher development, professional experience and building and maintaining university–school/community partnerships. She currently leads an Australian Government grant focused on improving the preparation of future teachers to work in partnership with Aboriginal and Torres Strait Islander parents and caregivers. Through her collective work, She aims to connect research, policy and practice in ways that bring teachers and school and university-based teacher educators together and break down traditional borders between academics, policymakers, communities and practitioners.

Peter Anderson is from the Walpiri and Murinpatha, First Nations in the Northern Territory. He is also an Associate Professor at Queensland University of Technology where he is the Director of the Indigenous Research and Engagement Unit. His research theorises the understandings of the organisational value of academic freedom in Australian universities and also more broadly in the polar south. His current research is in the areas of organisational leadership, indigenous peoples' education, and teacher and academic professional development. He currently leads an Australian government Special Research Initiative grant: the National Indigenous Research and Knowledges Network (NIRAKN). NIRAKN's vision is to develop a critical mass of skilled, informed and qualified Aboriginal and Torres Strait Islander researchers, who can address the urgent needs of our communities, through the delivery of culturally appropriate research. NIRAKN will endeavour to facilitate a national indigenous research agenda for Aboriginal and Torres Strait Islander communities and the nation.

Anna Darling is a Ph.D. candidate at the Faculty of Education, Monash University. Her study looks at the complexity of experiences of teacher educators in the spaces of Indigenous Education and Initial Teacher Education (ITE). Her research interests focus on the notions and practices of expertise, consultation, pedagogy and emotion in the space of Indigenous Education, and how these notions and practices are affected by education policies and university culture. She has contributed to research projects that investigate the barriers to effective preparation of pre-service teachers to undertake teaching placements in remote Aboriginal schools. Currently, she is working on two research projects that respectively examine the preparation of pre-service teachers to work in partnership with Aboriginal and Torres Strait Islander parents and caregivers, and explore the diversity and effectiveness of literacy programs in remote Aboriginal schools.

Chapter 9
Partnering with Schools Beyond Professional Experience: Building Equity-Centred ITE Programme Alignment and Coherence

Fiona Ell, Lexie Grudnoff, Mavis Haigh and Mary F. Hill

Abstract Uncertainty about teacher education around the world abounds as providers grapple with the challenge of preparing teachers who can foster the learning of increasingly diverse student populations. Hence, the policy focus in New Zealand, as in other nations, is on improving the quality of initial teacher education (ITE) through strengthening professional experience and school–university partnerships. This chapter reports a qualitative study that investigated how engagement in a school–university collaborative research project outside of ITE contributed to a New Zealand equity-centred teacher education programme's alignment and coherence. We interviewed teachers and teacher educators participating in the research project and teaching on the programme. Directed thematic data analysis identified three major themes—awareness, articulation and action. Using concepts from complexity theory, the study illustrates how building relationships with schools that extend beyond professional experience can occasion the emergence of deeper and shared understandings about practice for equity, reducing uncertainty and contributing to ITE programme alignment and coherence.

Keywords Initial teacher education · School–university partnerships
Equity · Complexity

F. Ell · L. Grudnoff (✉) · M. Haigh · M. F. Hill
The University of Auckland, Auckland, New Zealand
e-mail: l.grudnoff@auckland.ac.nz

F. Ell
e-mail: f.ell@auckland.ac.nz

M. F. Hill
e-mail: mf.hill@auckland.ac.nz

© Springer Nature Singapore Pte Ltd. 2018   129
D. Heck and A. Ambrosetti (eds.), *Teacher Education In and For Uncertain Times*,
https://doi.org/10.1007/978-981-10-8648-9_9

Introduction

Internationally, initial teacher education (ITE), particularly university-based ITE, faces uncertain times as it grapples with the challenge of preparing teachers who can foster the learning of increasingly diverse student populations (UNESCO, 2014). Additionally, ITE is increasingly being challenged to ensure that preservice teachers (PSTs) develop the knowledge and skills to teach in ways that address the problem of differential achievement between groups of students related to ethnicity, language, culture and gender. Given the prevalence of the education reform discourse that views educational underachievement as being a problem with teacher quality (Pullen, 2017), it is not surprising that teacher preparation has become the target of policymakers. For them, ITE is viewed as a key lever in the quest to improve student outcomes by improving teacher quality.

In many countries, policy initiatives have pushed ITE into taking a 'practice turn' (Reid, 2011) whereby greater value is placed on PSTs experiential learning in centre/school settings than on their campus-based learning. The 'practice turn', taken to its extreme, can be seen as a threat to tertiary study-based ITE and creates a sense of uncertainty for ITE providers. This 'turn' is evidenced in ITE policy reviews which demand that professional experience in ITE be strengthened. These include: Australia's Teacher Education Ministerial Advisory Group (TEMAG) report (2014) that amongst its 38 recommendations called for improved and structured practical experiences. England's Carter report (2015) called attention to improving the quality of school-led ITE by urging schools and ITE providers to work collaboratively to strengthen 'what has become a complex and sometimes a confusing system,' (p. 13). The Education Council of New Zealand's (2016) policy paper lists six future design principles for teacher education in New Zealand, including lifting the quality of the practicum through 'authentic partnerships between (schools/ECE centres that provide) the best possible mix of theory and practice' (para., 6).

While there is no doubt that professional experience is a vital part of ITE for PSTs and a quality teaching profession, more time in centres/schools does not necessarily lead to better student teacher learning (Grossman, 2010). It is therefore important that schools and universities work together to ensure that shared understanding of programme goals and expectations drive professional experience learning opportunities (Grudnoff, Haigh, & Mackisack, 2017b). This is in line with Le Cornu's (2015) argument that quality professional experience requires a high level of commitment from school leaders, high-quality mentor teachers and high-quality school–university partnerships. While partnerships between ITE and schools are not uncommon, McIntyre (2009) contended that often such partnerships focus on structural relationships and privilege university knowledge over practitioner expertise. Although relationships and partnerships are not the same thing, effective partnerships require sound relationships (Lefever-Davis, Johnson, & Pearman, 2007). It could thus be argued that the 'practice turn' is an opportunity for university ITE providers to develop richer and more authentically collaborative relationships with centres/schools.

Taking advantage of the 'practice turn' to enhance PST learning is not straight-forward given the complexity of relationships between universities and school sites in ITE (Cochran-Smith & Zeichner, 2005). Teacher education is complex in fundamental ways leading to nonlinear relationships between ITE activities and PST outcomes (Cochran-Smith et al., 2014). The complex nature of ITE means that if teacher educators want to shape the outcomes of teacher preparation in certain ways, they need to deliberately create the conditions from which more equitable outcomes are more likely to emerge (Davis & Sumara, 2006). This means more than making pragmatic changes: thought must be given to how ideas interact with each other to occasion the emergence of valued practice (Cochran-Smith et al., 2014; Davis & Sumara 2006, 2010).

Using complexity theory provides researchers with insights that are not apparent when linear ways of thinking are used (Davis & Sumara, 2010). Complexity theory is fundamentally a theory of learning and change (Mason, 2008), providing explanations for why unexpected consequences sometimes occur, why small changes might lead to large effects and why interventions may fail to make an impact (Byrne, 1998; Mason, 2008; Morrison, 2008). Complexity theory focuses on emergent phenomena and pays attention to the interactions and feedback mechanisms that occur within a complex system (Morrison, 2008). Complex systems are full of interdependencies and contingencies, the effects of which are non-random but unpredictable (Byrne, 1998; Cilliers, 1998; Waks, 2011). If we want to make change in a complex system (which educators do), we can use knowledge of how a complex system behaves to work out the most effective ways to intervene (Davis & Sumara, 2012). Complexity theory suggests that to promote emergence, ideas in a system need to recur and to 'bump up' against other ideas, ideally with a diversity of knowledge and experience present and some constraints around their use (Davis & Sumara, 2006). This chapter uses concepts from complexity theory to help us understand equity-centred teaching emerging from overlapping complex systems: a university ITE provider and two schools.

Context for the Study

Although the schools and the ITE programme had a history of working together, the relationships under investigation in this study were built through two parallel, linked initiatives. The first was a new post-graduate ITE programme at the Masters level where PSTs work in the schools for extended professional experience. The second initiative was a research project where the teachers and the teacher educators formed inquiry teams to research classroom practice. Both of these initiatives used 'facets of practice for equity', a set of key principles about teaching for equity, as the central organising framework.

Facets of Practice for Equity

The 'facets of practice for equity' were derived from a comparative synthesis of the literature on teaching that made a difference for all learners (Grudnoff et al., 2017a). The synthesis yielded six 'facets' that were further developed for use with PSTs and schools. The six facets are: (1) selecting worthwhile content and designing and implementing learning opportunities aligned to valued outcomes; (2) connecting to students as learners, their lives and experiences; (3) creating learning-focused, respectful and supportive learning environments; (4) using evidence to scaffold learning and improve teaching; (5) adopting an inquiry stance and taking responsibility for professional engagement and learning; and (6) recognising and seeking to address classroom, school and societal practices that reproduce inequity.

These six facets provide broad patterns of practice that have been empirically associated with improved social, academic, democratic and participatory outcomes for all learners. They are deliberately interdependent and described at the level of principle to maintain the fundamental complexity at the heart of teaching and learning, while providing direction as to what research suggests is fruitful facets of teaching and learning to attend to in teacher preparation. Enacting these facets of practice will look different in different contexts, so they do not specify exactly what to do or how to do it. Instead, the facets label overall intentions behind teaching actions so that PSTs can define the direction and purpose of their choices as they plan, teach and evaluate (Grudnoff et al., 2017a).

The Two Projects

The new ITE programme was a 1 year Masters of Teaching (Masters), deliberately designed to put 'equity front and center' (Nieto, 2000, p. 180), taught in collaboration with 12 primary partner schools with very diverse students in terms of culture, ethnicity, language and socioeconomic status. The Masters' PSTs encounter the facets of practice for equity on their first day and throughout all aspects of their one-year programme, using the facets as a lens to write assignments, understand new material and consider their practice. The facets are also part of assessing PSTs readiness to teach during professional experience (University of Auckland, 2017). PSTs spend two days per week based in a school and the other three days university-based. Courses are inquiry focused and integrate curriculum subjects.

A key feature of the Masters is the placement of PSTs in partner schools located in low socio-economic communities for three months in the final six months of the programme. Groups of 4–6 PSTs are assigned to schools and then placed in classrooms with associate teachers (mentors or cooperating teachers). A key teacher (adjunct lecturer) works with a university liaison lecturer to collaboratively construct the professional experience in each school. Schools that work in the Masters need to have a deep understanding of the programme's principles for the placement to be effective.

The second initiative was a New Zealand Ministry of Education funded Teaching, Learning and Research Initiative project, which focused on building knowledge about teaching in ways that promote equitable student outcomes. Two principals and seven teachers from two of the Masters' partner schools and five teacher educators established a collaborative inquiry community. In the first phase of this research project, the inquiry community collaborated to examine the facets of practice for equity, elaborating them by providing examples from practice and testing the research-derived ideas against the lived experience of the school participants. In the second phase, small inquiry teams were formed. Each team took a particular facet to examine in context and used a teacher inquiry model (Cochran-Smith & Lytle, 2009) to research the effects of a facet-based intervention.

Method

This paper is framed socioculturally (Wertsch, Del Rio, & Alvarez, 1995) and utilises a qualitative approach to reflexively capture participants' perspectives of the particular 'specific, delimited, local, historical situation' (Flick, 2006, p. 19). We wanted to capture the degree to which deeper school–university relationships resulting from co-engagement in the research project enabled members of the research team to better support the Masters' PSTs while they were undertaking professional experience. The research question for this study was: How, and in what ways, did the engagement of teachers and teacher educators in a collaborative inquiry community contribute to an equity-centred ITE programme's alignment and coherence?

Data sources included the audio recording of the research project's final meeting and interviews with members of the research team who had directly engaged with Masters' PSTs in schools. We interviewed two principals (Felicity and Georgie), two deputy principals who were adjunct lecturers for the Masters programme (Carolin and Penny), two associate teachers (Jenny and Kathy), one university liaison lecturer (Myra) and one teacher who had graduated from the Masters programme (Rebecca) [all pseudonyms]. While most were interviewed individually, the principal and deputy principal from one school were interviewed together. Interviews were of 30–40 min in duration and were audio-taped. Members of the research team who had not worked directly with Masters' PSTs during their extended professional experience were not interviewed individually for this study. We had previously received our university's Human Participants Research Ethics Committee approval for the research project and the participants' consent to interview all members of the research team as participants for research purposes.

We carried out two rounds of analysis of the interview data. First, we undertook a general thematic analysis (Braun & Clarke, 2013) following transcription. On completion of this analysis, we identified three higher level themes embedded in the data, and this led us to carry out a 'directed content analysis' (Hsieh & Shannon,

2005) to identify examples of these three themes. In the next section, we report on the findings from the directed content analysis, using examples and direct quotes provided by those interviewed.

Findings

The data suggested three ways in which the two schools' engagement in the Teaching, Learning and Research Initiative project appeared to increase ITE programme alignment and coherence and enhance the professional experience for the Masters' PSTs: awareness, articulation and action.

Awareness

The associate teachers explained how working with university-based team members as critical friends to unpack what the facets for equity meant in practice made them much clearer about what equity means and how it can be increased through the facets' lens. For example, Jenny (associate teacher) believed that 'the discussions we had (in the research project) about equity for our students made us much more aware, like hyper aware, of how we're including (school students) in our programme'. Kathy, also an associate teacher, agreed that participating in the research project led to 'being more aware of equity in class'. Penny, an adjunct lecturer, explained that:

> for myself, it's given me a greater understanding of what the facets were. We have been with the Masters programme (for three years) but I missed the first intake … so for me it's actually built my knowledge about what the facets are and what they look like in practice.

Participating in the research project had also made the teachers in these schools aware of differences between PSTs from different preparation programmes. The Masters' PSTs whose programme was underpinned by the facets of practice for equity could debate and discuss issues more deeply. As Carolin (adjunct lecturer) put it, 'I suppose they are more theoretical than the B.Ed. [Bachelor of Education students who complete a three-year course]. We have them together at the beginning … but the differences become very apparent … there's a difference in the way they think about equity'.

Rebecca, a graduate of the Masters who had been employed as a teacher at one of the schools and who participated in the research project, explained that because she had learnt to teach using the facets of practice for equity she now 'thinks about them naturally whereas they might be foreign to other people. It won't be difficult for us (who have been immersed in them) to discuss them because they are already in our minds'. Rebecca did, however, explain that when the facets were introduced on the very first day of her Masters programme, they seemed like a very big concept. 'The very first lecture we had was these (facets) so we were all, like, dumbfounded because it was all new. (But now) they are obviously inherent in what we do all the time, but the expression that they were going to cement our whole course, that was new!'

In one of the schools, Myra, a member of the collaborative research team, was the university liaison lecturer responsible for supervising the preservice teachers on professional experience. She had also been part of the team that developed both the Facets of Practice for Equity framework and the Masters ITE programme. Myra noticed that, compared with other associate teachers, the two associate teachers involved in the research project were much more aware of how they could use the facets to scaffold and model teaching for the PSTs. This became particularly obvious in the professional conversations held at the end of the placement.

Articulation

A second theme was the finding that having a common framework across the research project and the preservice programme appeared to facilitate discussion about equity issues between the PST and teachers within the two schools. In a clear example of this, Jenny described a discussion she had had with a Masters' PST in her class about the complex meanings related to equity:

> He and I had a really good discussion and we decided to agree not to agree. I take a gifted and talented group and he said that he felt that was making the inequity wider because those students were getting extra time when they were doing science with me every Tuesday afternoon. I said that for those children it's inequitable being in a normal room because they don't get access to that higher level of conversation they can get when they are with like-minded peers. I was able to use some of the wording and things that we (have discussed in the research project). I believe those kids need that opportunity. (Jenny, Associate Teacher)

Articulating aspects of the facets of practice for equity was another benefit of participating in both the research project and the preparation programme. Carolin, in her role as adjunct lecturer, met every Friday afternoon with all five PSTs placed in her school for the three months of extended professional experience. On the suggestion of their school's university liaison lecturer, Carolin had encouraged discussion and dialogue:

> It created these amazing discussions around the things they had seen or done or been part of in terms of the facets and also providing equitable outcomes for all and how challenging that is …. They bring the things … that they see. We did an assessment one (discussion) and how fair it was if they couldn't speak English. And we talked about a child not having access to the same things on a trip because they were in a wheelchair. I think it's [the facets framework] a good framework for discussion … seeing how they all intertwine. (Carolin, Adjunct Lecturer)

Towards the end of the extended placement, professional conversations were held between each Masters' PST, the associate teacher, adjunct lecturer, university liaison lecturer and the school principal. The purpose was to give PSTs the opportunity to demonstrate and discuss how they had met their professional experience goals.

Myra, the university liaison lecturer, noticed that those PSTs with associate teachers in the research project articulated their progress in terms of the facets of practice and equity to a far greater extent than those whose associate teachers had not been part of the research project. The associate teachers also noticed the use of the framework in discussions about goals and planning. For example, '... (The PSTs) ... shared their goals re the facets we are looking at and we would choose to work on those as well as doing an inquiry' (Kathy, associate teacher).

A greater ease around articulating practices associated with equity, leading to the modelling of practice for equity to the Masters' PSTs, was acknowledged by one of the principals as an outcome of engagement in the research project. She indicated that 'It was [always] about articulating the way it is around here. However, our discussions have become more formal after the discussions that we had in the project' (Felicity, Principal). There was also recognition that even if a teacher had difficulty explaining the facets, their behaviour would exemplify their understanding: 'I think that what we would be looking for most is living the facets. If you can't explain what they are, your behaviour will show that you get it' (Penny, adjunct lecturer).

Two participants gave examples of further ways in which they had come to have the understanding and use the vocabulary with PSTs while on placement. Rebecca, a graduate of the Masters programme, explained that working in the research project and with PSTs was natural because she knew the facets from her preservice programme. In addition to being involved in the research project, Carolin had encountered the facets of practice for equity and inquiry research when she had attended the ITE Masters' professional learning workshop days at the university. As she said,

> I've attended all the Masters Teaching days so I'm part of all that stuff. I go when they meet so I know a lot more on top of, you know I've been there for their discussions and stuff and I think that helps too. If you said they're learning about this, this is what they're doing at uni and I read through it and think oh yeah but because I've done the research it ties into what I know at uni so it kind of brings it all together. I don't think I'd be as confident to talk to them with them (PSTs) about it, if I hadn't done the research. (Carolin, Adjunct Lecturer)

Being aware of the facets of practice for equity and using these to discuss planning and practice led to the third theme in the findings, putting the ideas into action.

Action

Putting understandings of facets of practice for equity into action occurred in several different ways. Firstly, the associate teachers who understood the Masters' framework were able to help PSTs understand the principles in practice by modelling such practice. One associate teacher (Kathy) described how she had specifically and consciously modelled facet 2 (*Connecting to students as learners, and to their lives and experiences*) as she worked with three challenging boys who were continually off task. Together with her PST, she sought to understand these boys as learners and to find out what their particular interests were. As a result, the PST selected reading books and prepared activities around the topic of bikes for one of these boys with the result that *'he really took off '*.

Another associate teacher (Jenny) was able to model to her PST how she responded to facet 6 (*Recognising and seeking to address, classroom, school and societal practices that reproduce inequity*) when she was planning a field trip to an island bird sanctuary for her senior primary school students. One of the children in her class used a wheel chair, and the schools' initial response was that she may not be able to go on the trip. However, triggered by consideration of facet 6, Jenny planned ways the child could be included in the trip, preparing the island rangers ahead of time and ensuring that ramps would be available to enable her to participate fully in this important learning experience.

The Masters' PSTs had also been able to act on the facets following leads by adjunct lecturers and university liaison lecturers. For example, Carolin, as an adjunct lecturer, reflected that during one of the Friday afternoon PST discussions early in the extended professional experience, one PST, Meredith, lamented that her 10-year old students were not engaged in her maths lessons. Carolin and the university liaison lecturer asked her why she thought that was and suggested she think about her students, their lives and experiences (facet 2) in connection with the maths tasks she was offering. Meredith decided to find some Samoan stories and events to use as the context for the tasks. Carolin observed that at next Friday's PST discussion Meredith was very upbeat. Her problem-based maths lesson had been very successful, engaging her students and holding their interest. Carolin talked about how the discussion that afternoon expanded into ways the other PSTs could develop similar strategies.

Another action resulting from engagement in the research project was enhanced support for the PSTs as they carried out an inquiry-oriented research project that was a capstone requirement for the Masters ITE programme. One adjunct lecturer described how, as she had carried out the facet-framed inquiry that was part of the research project, she had:

> … built my knowledge about the inquiry process, I guess it deepened my knowledge about the inquiry process and the sort of things the Masters' PSTs are coming to us with and what we have to work with. So I guess also going through this project is being able to help myself with [understanding inquiry], I mean I have an inquiry mind-set, but actually getting into the mind-set of what the Masters people should come out, look like, and work to the level—what you can expect of them. (Penny, Adjunct Lecturer)

The Principal in this school commented that the other research project-linked teachers in her school were well into their inquiry but thought 'it will be a bit of work for other teachers just to bring them over to this way of thinking … when we work with the new associate teachers, we are trying to recruit at the moment' (Felicity, Principal).

Another action involved preparation of associate teachers to work with Masters' PSTs. Penny, who had this responsibility as an adjunct lecturer, commented:

> Making the transition from the sort of work we've been doing with the facets [in the research project], to working with a new group of associate teachers, I think a better understanding for myself of what the facets are [is aiding me] actually helps teachers come on board …

connecting what they do with a framework like facets when it is put in front of them. (Penny, Adjunct Lecturer)

The value of working collaboratively in the research team and the enhanced alignment of the ITE programme resulting from this were summed up by the other Principal:

I think there are huge gains from working with each other because we do learn from each other ... We might have Masters PSTs working on inquiry when they come into the school and the associates might be working in the old ways. It could be a real mismatch. (Georgie, Principal)

Discussion

Partnership between university ITE providers and schools is often presented as a solution to the perceived 'problems' of ITE, in particular, that ITE is too theoretical and irrelevant to practice settings (Cochran-Smith & Zeichner, 2005). This study provides insights into how establishing professional relationships with schools that extend beyond ITE can enhance teacher preparation and demonstrates how university providers and schools can each offer the other valuable knowledge and insights when collaborative relationships are established and mutually valued (Le Cornu, 2015).

In this study, the facets of practice for equity provided a common language between the two initiatives (the ITE Masters programme and the research project) and acted as a framework for developing the teacher educators', teachers' and PSTs understandings of teaching for equity and understandings of each other (Grudnoff et al., 2017b). As such, the facets often acted as a prompt for teacher and PST thinking and as a framework for professional discussion and assessment. Without involvement in the research project, we believe the teachers would not have engaged with the facets in such depth, and they would have remained 'university criteria' rather than being something recognised and valued by the teachers. In the first phase of the research project the teachers were positioned as experts, being consulted by the university researchers to enrich the researchers' understanding of the facets. This combining of perspectives flowed into the teachers' practice with PSTs, where the teachers were confident in their knowledge of the facets and able to use them to 'talk the same talk' as the PSTs. This led to richer feedback to PSTs and deeper conversations as both PSTs and teachers had a framework for deciding what mattered in their practice if they wanted to improve equity.

Complexity theory offers constructs that give insight into how a list of six facets could cause learning and change in practice for PSTs, teachers and teacher educators. Davis and Sumara (2006) offer three conditions that underpin emergence (which in this case is the emergence of practice that improves equity). These three paired conditions help explain emergence. The Masters and the research project intiatives were both designed to make use of these complexity learning ideas to occasion the emergence of deeper understanding about practice for equity.

The first condition is 'diversity-redundancy'. The diversity of ideas and perspectives in a system defines what the system has to work with; 'diversity in any complex learning system is, in essence, the source of its intelligence' (Davis & Sumara, 2010, p. 858). If the participants in a system all know and believe the same things, the system has narrow parameters to work with. Increasing diversity increases the opportunity for new ideas to emerge that go beyond any individual person's knowledge or experience. Redundancy, the condition where there is shared knowledge, language or ideas in many parts of the system is, however, also 'vital to system coherence' (Davis & Sumara, 2010, p. 858). Redundancy in the system makes the utilisation of diversity possible. In this study, the facets provided redundancy, appearing across both projects. Diversity was provided by the differing perspectives of the teacher educators, teachers and PSTs. This combination provided the conditions for rich learning about practice for equity.

The second condition is 'enabling constraints' (Davis & Sumara, 2006). If the conditions for emergence are unrestrained, then less learning occurs than if some boundaries are provided. The provision of basic 'rules of engagement' within systems opens spaces for creativity and development of new ideas. In these projects, the inquiry process and the facets provided constraints that enabled new understandings to emerge. Both the PSTs and the teachers undertook inquiry projects underpinned by the facets, and the inquiry process constrained their learning activity by defining phases and providing accountability. This opened a professional learning space (Timperley, Kaser, & Halbert, 2014) in which PSTs and teachers learned about teaching for equity.

The third condition describes the way that interaction takes place in the learning system. Interaction and feedback are the means by which complex systems learn and change. Davis and Sumara (2006) highlight the frequency of 'neighbour interactions' as fundamental to learning in a complex system, and pair this with 'decentralised control', a state in which hierarchies of power do not control the flow of ideas, and new learning can emerge from the participants through their interactions. While this may sound like people in the system interacting with each other, it also (and perhaps more fundamentally) applies to the neighbour interactions between ideas, which can be deliberately made to 'bump into' each other by being juxtaposed and to decentralised control over which ideas are legitimated and promulgated in the system. As an interdependent set of ideas, the facets promote neighbour interactions, where the concepts within each facet come up against each other, and against ideas about the facets in the university and the practice settings (Davis & Sumara, 2006). Collaboration between the teacher, Principals and university-based teacher educators decentralised control of the ideas and increased the likelihood of 'neighbour interactions' between ideas and perspectives. This led to an enriched understanding of teaching for equity for all participants.

These three ideas from complexity theory help to theorise the phenomenon that we observed; that working with schools on the research project and in ITE, centred on key ideas, can result in enhanced experiences for PSTs, and for university and school-based teacher educators. Davis and Sumara (2012) present the idea of a 'partner research school' as a way to legitimise and include the knowledge and expertise of all those involved in ITE. This study describes a successful example of this approach.

Conclusion

The 'practice turn' in ITE challenges tertiary ITE providers to form productive professional relationships, and then partnerships, with practice settings—and to do so in a way that preserves a role for what tertiary providers can contribute. Internationally, the proliferation of alternate route and 'school direct' models of teacher preparation creates uncertainty about the contribution of university-based ITE. Schools and centres themselves sometimes add to this rhetoric—as do PSTs who report that they find elements of their preparation 'useless'. This chapter presents a possibility for ITE providers to consider: working with schools/centres in ways that extend beyond professional experience arrangements to provide a common language and set of ideas for thinking about teacher practice more broadly. Though too small to warrant generalisations, this study suggests that such partnerships can provide opportunities to build deep and shared understandings of teaching and learning, which, in turn, can facilitate rich PST professional practice learning opportunities (Davis & Sumara, 2012).

The facets of practice for equity were central to developing deep and shared understandings in this study. As understanding of the facets became shared amongst the school and university participants, the contributions of both parties to the development of PSTs practice for equity became clearer. In contrast to school–university partnerships built around structural considerations (McIntyre, 2009), this study suggests that discussing and elaborating key ideas, rather than pragmatics, may be a powerful way to extend relationships and reduce uncertainty about the role of ITE providers in twenty-first century ITE.

References

Braun, V., & Clarke, V. (2013). *Successful qualitative research: A practical guide for beginners*. London: Sage.

Byrne, D. (1998). *Complexity theory and the social sciences*. London, UK: Routledge.

Carter, A. (2015). *Review of initial teacher training (ITT)*. Downloaded from www.gov.uk/government/publications.

Cilliers, P. (1998). *Complexity and postmodernism: Understanding complex systems*. London, UK: Routledge.

Cochran-Smith, M., & Lytle, S. (2009). *Inquiry as stance: Teacher research for the next generation*. New York: Teachers College Press.

Cochran-Smith, M., & Zeichner, K. (Eds.). (2005). *Studying teacher education: The report of the AERA panel on research and teacher education*. Mahwah, New Jersey: American Educational Research Association and Lawrence Erlbaum Associates.

Cochran-Smith, M., Ell, F., Ludlow, L., Grudnoff, L., Haigh, M., & Hill, M. (2014). When complexity theory meets critical realism: A platform for research on initial teacher education. *Teacher Education Quarterly, 41*(1), 105–122.

Davis, B., & Sumara, D. (2006). *Complexity and education: Inquiries into learning, teaching, and research.* Mahwah, NJ: Erlbaum.

Davis, B., & Sumara, D. (2010). "If things were simple …": Complexity in education. *Journal of Evaluation in Clinical Practice, 16,* 856–860.

Davis, B., & Sumara, D. (2012). Fitting teacher education in/to/for an increasingly complex world. *Complicity, 9*(1), 30–40.

Education Council. (2016) *Strategic options for developing future oriented initial teacher education.* Downloaded from https://educationcouncil.org.nz.

Flick, U. (2006). *An introduction to qualitative research.* London: Sage.

Grossman, P. (2010). *Learning to practice: The design of clinical experiences in teacher preparation.* Washington, DC: American Association of Colleges for Teacher Education & National Education Association.

Grudnoff, L., Haigh, M., Hill, M. F., Cochran-Smith, M., Ell, F., & Ludlow, L. (2017a). Teaching for equity: Insights from international evidence. *The Curriculum Journal, 28*(3), 305–326. https://doi.org/10.1080/09585176.2017.1292934.

Grudnoff, L., Haigh, M., & Mackisack, V. (2017b). Re-envisaging and reinvigorating school-university practicum partnerships. *Asia-Pacific Journal of Teacher Education, 45*(2), 180–193. https://doi.org/10.1080/1359866X.2016.1201043.

Hsieh, H.-F., & Shannon, S. (2005). Three approaches to qualitative content analysis. *Qualitative Health Research, 15*(9), 1277–1288.

Le Cornu, R. (2015). *Key components of effective professional experience in initial teacher education in Australia.* A paper prepared for the Australian Institute for Teaching and School Leadership, Melbourne.

Lefever-Davis, S., Johnson, C., & Pearman, C. (2007). Two sides of a partnership: Egalitarianism and empowerment in school-university partnerships. *The Journal of Educational Research, 100*(4), 204–210.

Mason, M. (Ed.). (2008). *Complexity theory and the philosophy of education.* West Sussex, UK: Wiley Blackwell.

McIntyre, D. (2009). The difficulties of inclusive pedagogy for initial teacher education and some thoughts on the way forward. *Teachers and Teacher Education, 25,* 602–608.

Morrison, K. (2008). Educational philosophy and the challenge of complexity theory. In M. Mason (Ed.), *Complexity theory and the philosophy of education* (pp. 16–31). West Sussex, UK: Wiley Blackwell.

Nieto, S. (2000). Placing equity front and center: Some thoughts on transforming teacher education for a new century. *Journal of Teacher Education, 51*(3), 180–187.

Pullen, D. (2017). What counts? Who is counting? Teacher education improvement and accountability in a data-driven era. In J. Nuttall, A. Kostogriz, M. Jones, & J. Martin (Eds.), *Teacher education policy and practice: Evidence of impact, impact of evidence* (pp. 3–16). Singapore: Springer.

Reid, J. A. (2011). A practice turn for teacher education? *Asia-Pacific Journal of Teacher Education, 39*(4), 293–310.

Teacher Education Ministerial Advisory Group [TEMAG]. (2014). *Action now: Classroom ready teachers.* Retrieved from https://www.studentsfirst.gov.au/teacher-education-ministerial-advisory-group.

Teaching and Learning Research Initiative. (n.d.). Home page http://tlri.org.nz/.

Timperley, H., Kaser, L., & Halbert, J. (2014). A framework for transforming learning in schools: Innovation and the spiral, *Seminar series: Vol. 234.* Melbourne: Centre for Strategic Education.

UNESCO. (2014). Teaching and learning: Achieving quality for all, EFA Global Monitoring Report. Paris, France: UNESCO Publishing.

University of Auckland, Faculty of Education and Social Work. (2017). *Master of teaching EDPROF 758: Inquiring into practice*. Auckland, NZ: Author.

Waks, L. (2011). Teacher education programs as complex organizations. *Emerging Changes in Teacher Education, 8*(1), 65–69.

Wertsch, J., Del Rio, P., & Alvarez, A. (Eds.). (1995). *Sociocultural studies of the mind*. Cambridge, UK: Cambridge University Press.

Author Biographies

Fiona Ell is an Associate Professor and Associate Dean ITE in the Faculty of Education and Social Work at the University of Auckland. She began her career as a primary school teacher before moving into teacher education and research. Fiona's research is concerned with how people learn in complex social settings, such as schools, universities and communities. She is involved in several national and international research projects that are investigating different elements of how new understandings, ideas and attitudes are developed and adopted by teachers and teacher candidates. Fiona is fundamentally interested in the practice of teaching and the experience of learning, and tries to keep her research focused on questions that will improve educational outcomes for all learners.

Lexie Grudnoff is an Associate Professor in the Faculty of Education and Social Work at the University of Auckland, New Zealand. She is the past chair of the Teacher Education Forum of Aotearoa New Zealand (TEFANZ) and has had extensive experience in the design, implementation, and evaluation of ITE programmes. Lexie researches and publishes in the area of new teacher professional learning. She is co-leader of a US-NZ research group that is using a complexity-critical realism framework to investigate how, and to what extent, PST learn to engage in patterns of teaching practice that supports all students' learning and challenge educational inequities. Lexie teaches and supervises postgraduate students' research in areas related to initial teacher education and beginning teaching.

Mavis Haigh recently retired as an Associate Professor at the Faculty of Education and Social Work, University of Auckland, New Zealand and is now an Honorary Research Fellow. She was a secondary science teacher before becoming a teacher educator and academic. Her research interests include teachers'/teacher educators' work, professional practice in initial teacher education, the assessment of student teachers' practice and the integration of complexity theory and critical realism as an explanatory theory for rethinking teacher education for equity. Her publications have included articles focusing on fostering creativity in science education, preparing teachers to teach aspects of the nature of science to both secondary and primary-aged learners and using social judgment theory to make judgments regarding pre-service teachers' readiness to teach.

Mary F. Hill is an Associate Professor at the Faculty of Education and Social Work, University of Auckland, New Zealand. She was a primary school teacher and deputy principal before becoming a teacher educator and academic. Her work is grounded in the context of contemporary schooling and teacher education, and the contribution that quality teaching makes to a socially just society. Her research interests include teachers'/teacher educators' work, educational assessment, practitioner inquiry and the use of complexity theory and critical realism as an explanatory theory for rethinking teacher education for equity. She has published evidence-based chapters, articles and books related to teacher professional development in formative assessment practices, including preparing teachers to use assessment to accelerate learning and increase equity of schooling outcomes.

Lightning Source UK Ltd.
Milton Keynes UK
UKHW02n1501180418
321277UK00003B/87/P